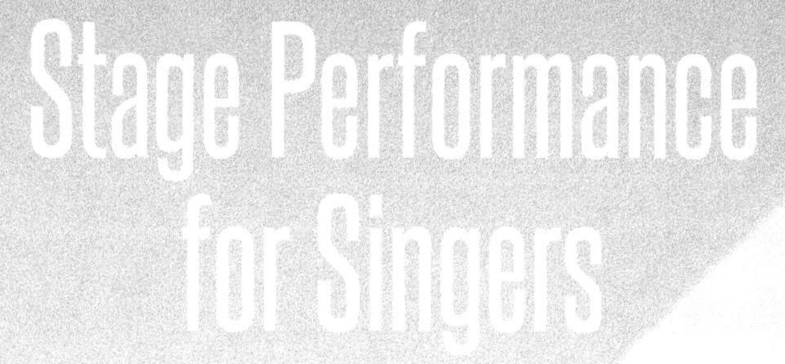

Stage Performance for Singers

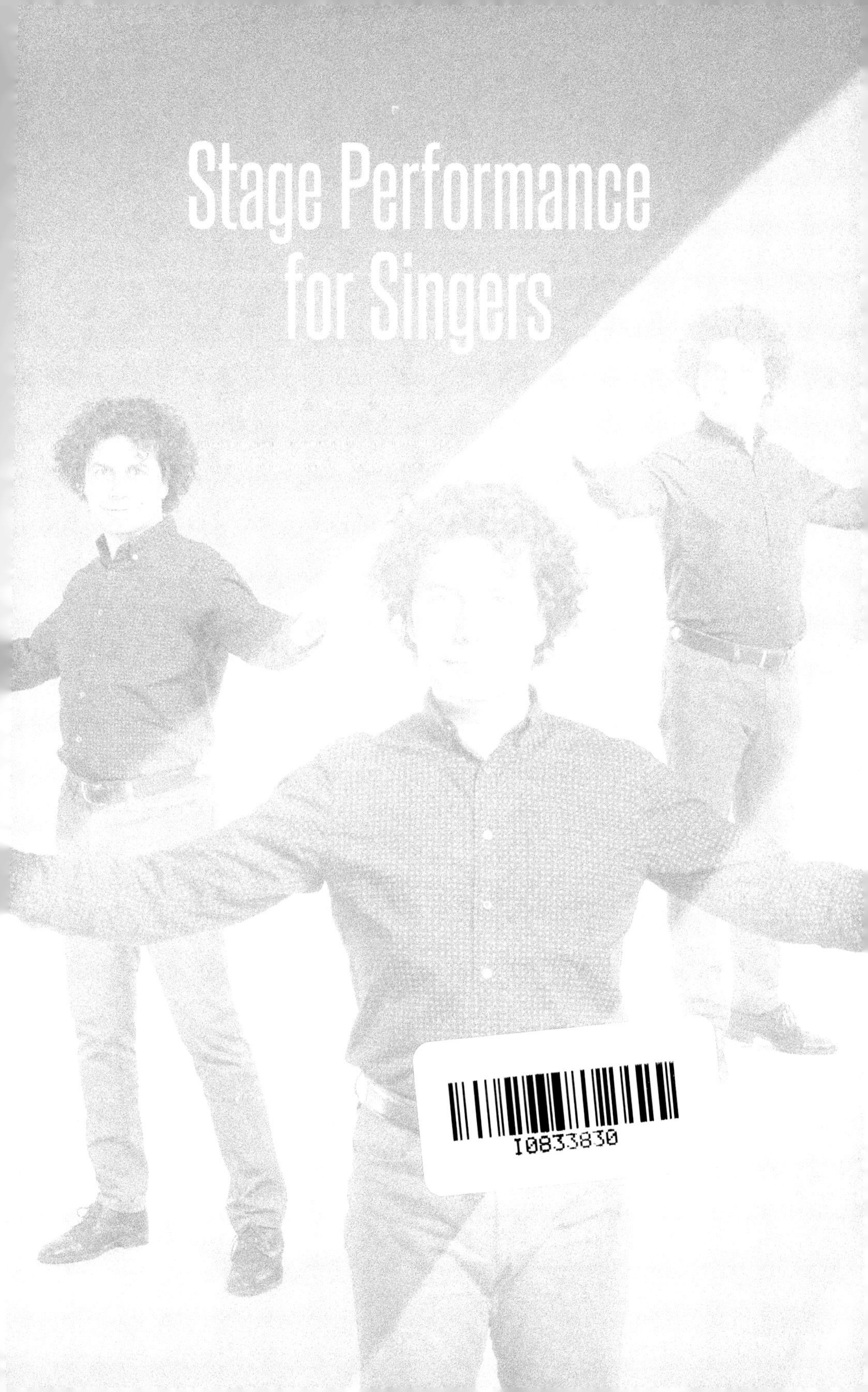

Stage Performance for Singers

A Practical Course in 12 Basic Steps

Martin Karnolsky

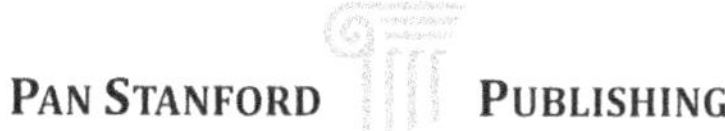
Pan Stanford Publishing

Published by

Pan Stanford Publishing Pte. Ltd.
Penthouse Level, Suntec Tower 3
8 Temasek Boulevard
Singapore 038988

Email: editorial@panstanford.com
Web: www.panstanford.com

British Library Cataloguing-in-Publication Data
A catalogue record for this book is available from the British Library.

Stage Performance for Singers: A Practical Course in 12 Basic Steps

ISBN 978-981-4800-20-4 (Paperback)
ISBN 978-0-429-42869-2 (eBook)

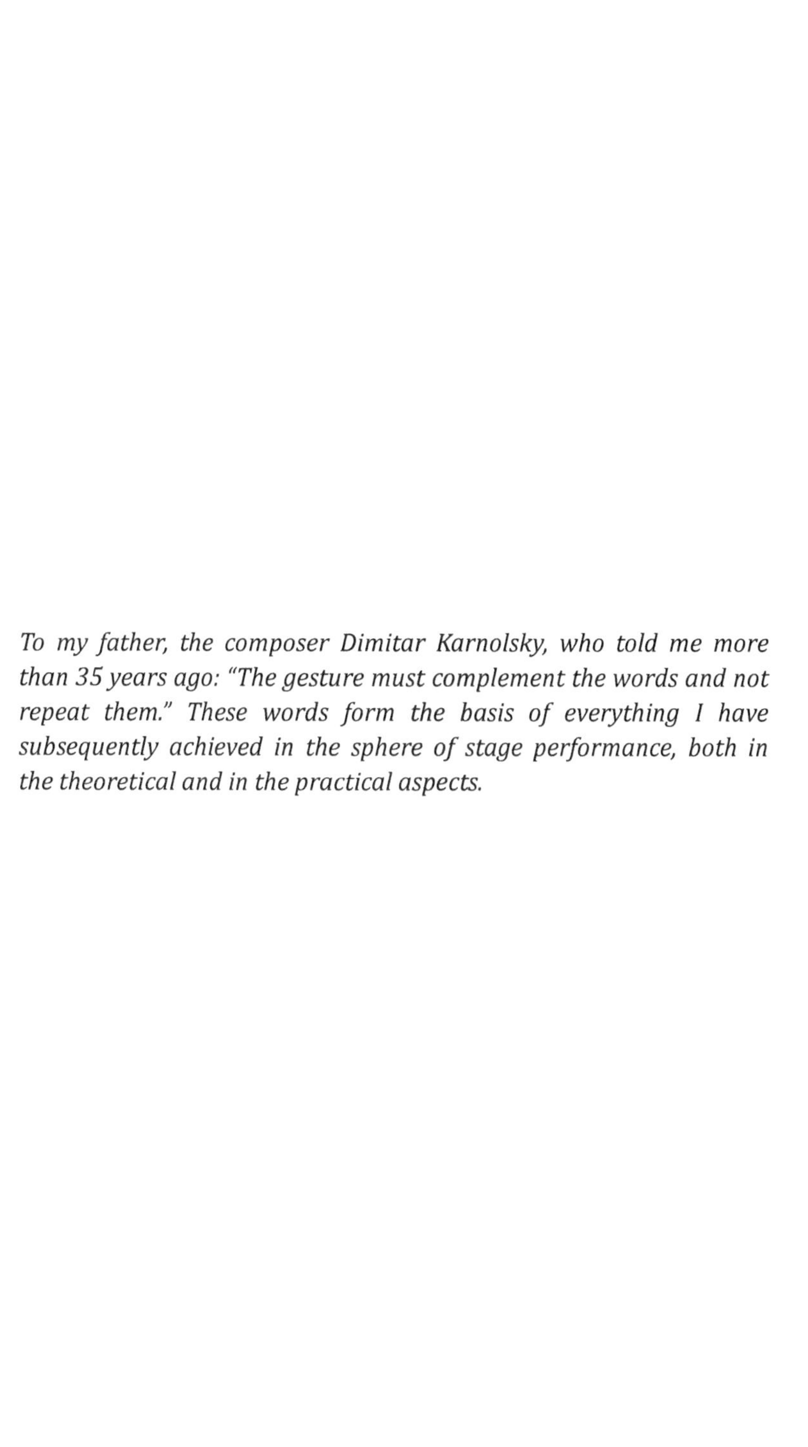

To my father, the composer Dimitar Karnolsky, who told me more than 35 years ago: "The gesture must complement the words and not repeat them." These words form the basis of everything I have subsequently achieved in the sphere of stage performance, both in the theoretical and in the practical aspects.

Contents

Introduction

Not everything is as complicated as it may seem. However, the contrary is also true. I am writing this book with the purpose of provoking the people who believe that walking out on the stage and singing a song is already a sign of success in itself. I am also writing for those for whom walking on stage and singing a song with their eyes closed and the microphone held in both hands is a heroic deed and unique in its artistry. And also for those who wish to achieve a bit more than holding the mike's 'head' and making infinite repetitions of the same gestures with hands in their pockets and eyes fixed on the floor or on the sky. Of course, I am also addressing those who do nothing of the above and do not know what to do at all. I am writing for vocal pedagogues, for students in all genres of singing, as well as for people who would like to go deeper into the techniques of correct and esthetic behavior and natural contact with the audience.

What should one expect from this text dedicated to stage performance? These are 12 basic steps any person should know when walking out on stage. These are approaches to the subject of stage performance from the last 20 years, put together and organized in this book. They represent my conclusions based on careful analysis of a number of successful and unsuccessful stage performances of singers of different statures. What we will actually do is study how to communicate with the audience.

I believe that every person is born with some knowledge and knows more than what this book may offer. However, I also believe that reading what I have rendered systematic here, will make it easier to achieve that coveted success. At least this is what my experience tells me.

I wish you interesting moments with *Stage Performance for Singers* and hope that each and every one of you will discover something personally valuable in this book. This will vindicate my work and please me enormously.

Chapter 1

Preparation and Beginning of Performance

In this chapter you will learn of the basic positions in the preparation for singing one or several songs, pieces, or a whole concert. You will also learn when the performance of a piece or a concert starts and ends. I will deal with preparation for a *concert* or *concert performance* as an important aspect of the perfect performer's delivery. This subject is as important as the other aspects examined in this book. Practically, everyone should know that a system composed of different elements is as strong as its weakest element. That is, we must not underestimate any aspect of our preparation, the actual performance on the stage, and our behavior after it. All these elements are of absolute importance!

The preparation for the performance includes all preliminary work in the rehearsal hall, working with designers, photographers and others, and it may last for weeks or months. This is besides the specific actions before the concert appearance. If we agree that everything that needs to be done in the course of the preliminary stages of the preparation is completed and we already are on the concert platform or in the hall, let us discuss what

Stage Performance for Singers: A Practical Course in 12 Basic Steps
Martin Karnolsky

ISBN 978-981-4800-20-4 (Paperback), 978-0-429-42869-2 (eBook)
www.panstanford.com

needs to be done right before the concert. This includes locating the spot where the actor can get ready without distraction, at least as far as this is possible. In the dressing room the makeup, hairstyle, change of costumes and small, last moment adjustments as well as other seemingly insignificant things are done. This is the place where the actor arranges his thoughts and focuses before stepping on the stage. This is where he rehearses a text or choreography or warms up his voice. When does the performance begin? I always ask this question and expect every actor to formulate the answer for himself. I have heard an endless number of answers. Starting from "When we start singing" to "At the moment when we took the decision to sing this particular song." I categorically disagree with the first answer. We cannot step onto the stage featuring the staggering walk of a sailor and when the moment of singing comes, to turn into the princess for which we have dressed up. Please note that I am talking about US, as I rank myself among the creative and artistic people and have often been on stage in different roles. We should "be" in character long before the singing starts. It is not by accident that I ask the question on when our performance should begin. Certainly not when our singing takes off.

I can agree with the second somewhat extreme answer, but with an additional reservation which may slightly alter the real essence of the question. If at the very moment when we decide which song to perform, we are ready with everything needed to walk on stage and give a brilliant performance, then we belong to the category of the super genius who also possesses elements of clairvoyance and unlimited abilities. The decision to take a step is not the actual step. From a philosophical point of view it is important that we visualize the goal from the very first moment. It is important that we have a vision of what we want to achieve. However, this does not mean that we are ready. Not at all! If we do not know where we are heading, we may not get anywhere!

The truth is that the performance starts before our appearance on stage. This is the moment when we stand quietly backstage and wait to be announced. A short time before the moment of the announcement, the artist must remember the important things, the basic points on which his character is built. He remembers the lyrics, music, dance steps and, when announced, he is already in character. I refer you once more to the "sailor with the princess costume." No! This is absurd, to run to the microphone or walk as someone ready to fight and turn into something very different once you have reached the place. What we must simply do is show with our first step on stage that we are actors and will now tell a story, be it joyful, sad, heroic, a ballad or a charade. If this does not happen—we are late! We have missed the moment of the first impression. Based on the remarks above, I would like to draw your attention to a fact proven by scientists.

Research on body language tells us that when we meet someone for the first time, we create up to 90%, even 95% of our impression of a particular person during the first 90 seconds of our first meeting (see Allan Pease and Alan Garner, *Body Language. Talk Language*). It is crucial to know that, to remember it and take it into consideration when we make our first step on the stage for a performance. This is also true about our performance. The audience is watching us and the moment we appear on stage people form their opinion about us. They see everything. *everything*! Our costume, how we walk, how we move our hands, what we look at, how we hold the microphone, besides our makeup and so much more. We, people, understand body language, but only a few can *speak* body language. It is like a language close to our native one, which we understand but cannot speak. Do not forget this! Great attention must always be paid to our first appearance, to the first tones if singing, to the first words if speaking. They create the first impression about us and it stays longer than a moment. It is there during the whole performance on the stage on the day and after it. We study how to communicate with the audience in the most natural of ways. And we do that throughout our artistic lives. This is the purpose of the book you are holding in your hands—to provoke a striving after natural communication with the audience and the reader. Without unnecessary distractions or insufficiencies.

So far I have drawn your attention to when our performance begins in case of one, two or more songs in a concert with more participants. Actually, several songs constitute a mini concert.

Further, we will discuss what happens and what we do when we have to perform more than one song *en bloc*. That is, when our next performance starts we are on the stage and have sung the first number.

The most interesting aspect in this case is the quick transition from one character into another. Preparation for the next performance in mere seconds. Preparing not only ourselves, but also the audience. To make it in such a way that everything around us on the stage looks natural. We also need to look natural during the transition from one character into another.

It is time to note that the vision for our performance as a whole is of exceptional importance. Arranging the program to make it interesting, developing and leading to a natural culmination includes thinking about a number of other things too. One of them is costume. We will dwell on that further on. For now we just have to note that our general approach should be to select a costume which will correspond to the specific location and event. It also needs to be sufficiently multifunctional, thus being suitable for all the songs in the mini concert. Well, if we talk about a big individual concert (may God bless us all), then we need to think about where, when and how to allot time to change.

Let us go back to the mini concert. The beginning has been clarified. We start when we are announced. We have embraced the first character. We go on stage and sing our number. We make a bow. A short pause. It is fine to say a few words. If this is not possible or the director (or somebody else) does not allow us to talk, then we need to find a way to smoothly transit from one character into another. What do I mean by smooth transition? One option is simply to take a pause. Make an invisible to the audience gesture to the sound engineer, the conductor or to the accompanying group to say you are ready for the next song. I actually mean to say that you need to give the audience a chance to take a breath. Also, to evaluate what they have listened to. Give them a chance to enjoy your performance. This is a process the mastery of which comes with practice. We need to know when the audience is ready for our next performance. Most probably this is the moment when the applause calms down and subsides. What about for the stars when the audience will simply *not stop* cheering? We can only rely on our personal judgement! Be careful and do not impose your personal rhythm at any cost. Try to respect the audience and its pulse. Try to learn how to "breathe" with the audience. When you can feel that the audience is ready to listen to the next song, go ahead.

I would like to refer to something mentioned above—the costume. If the program requires a change of costume, we need to think about the so called "universal" costume, which will allow a change of our appearance with small and quick touches. Taking off a hat, a wig, a part of the costume—a jacket or a shawl—or taking a flower in your hand may be very helpful in making the transition to the next song smooth and what is most important—make it understandable to the audience.

Now let us look at the individual concert. What are our problems? Besides changing costumes, position on the stage, perhaps dancing the ballet. Actually, everything may happen during an individual concert. Well, let us see what the basic problems are. We need to think about what to do in the course of performing the songs, besides thinking about this big form, the development, culmination and finale. Definitely, decisions on the costume, light, special effects, etc. will be taken with the assistance of the relevant specialists. We also need to consider the intervals, the places where we change or simply set apart time for musicians, a ballet dancer or another participant in the concert to perform, so that we can have a break. What remains is basically the same—a smooth or abrupt transition to the next character. Changing the costume, taking off part of it, adding something. Also, by all means, a finale with well-thought-through long but not tedious bows and receiving an ovation. An encore, would be great! It depends on us. Also, I am not joking about something which "is known to everybody and does not need to be repeated once again!"

The encore is the perfection each concert performer must achieve and know how "to deserve it." This may sound abstract, even extravagant, but the truth is that if you do not program your performances at the concert in a way which will lead to a natural culmination of the whole project, if they are not shorter or longer than expected, if the whole presentation is not good or excellent, the audience will not ask for an encore! You can be sure of that! You must learn to direct and why not?—manipulate people. Lead them from one place to another in your own way! This happens, however, by knowing all aspects of your performance and by preparing for it.

Conclusion

Our single performance or concert is prepared in the rehearsal hall. Each element needs prior planning and preparation: the repertoire, the order of delivering the repertoire, the histrionics, the dialogue delivery, the modulations and everything that goes with them. The beginning of the performance starts when the announcer has declared your name and you are backstage. The actor gets ready and focuses. The end of the performance is once again backstage—while walking out of the stage you are still in character.

Chapter 2

Stage Space Split

In this chapter you will learn about the physical split of the stage space, about the important location spots, as well as where and how the actor should position himself on the stage.

The stage is our home, our working place, or pedestal and magic—we own all that and the audience *does not*! This is where the magic key is hidden—we *master* it! Dominating the stage is an obligatory skill to be learnt by anyone stepping on the stage in order to sing, dance, speak, offer bouquets or present an award. What is the stage? This is the space given to us to perform our art—in our case these are songs and their accompanying arts and artistic means. The stage has the "effect of the frame"—"all within it is clearly and distinctly visible as if under a magnifying glass" (M. Frish).

Before discussing the actual distribution of the stage space, it is relevant to note what is on, around and above it. Scenography, sound and light equipment, podia, stairs, stands for musical instruments and microphones, as well as the instruments themselves may be on the stage. The theatrical scenery may be made of wood, metal, fabrics and other materials which impart the stage with brilliance and beauty and renders the general

Stage Performance for Singers: A Practical Course in 12 Basic Steps
Martin Karnolsky

ISBN 978-981-4800-20-4 (Paperback), 978-0-429-42869-2 (eBook)
www.panstanford.com

idea of the event. It also recreates the epoch to which the event is dedicated.

Next to the stage or around it there will usually be "sleeves" or "pockets." This is the case of stages of the "theatrical" type. But if we are on an open stage, there will be steps, advertising boards and what not. Or there may be nothing of that. Behind the stage there is most often the "back." It may carry advertising on it or it may simply be covered with black or some other cloth. In a third case it may just be a video screen. Many more variants are possible. The light equipment is usually situated above the stage. Often the sound equipment is at the very front. Or it is hung in the air—on the lights control console or on something else. Sometimes large screens may be placed on both sides at the front.

Everything said so far refers to what is most often in front of, behind, around, or above the stage. Participants can arrange the stage according to their preferences. There are concerts in which the stage has no back but only a front. Or it is the front from all sides. These are the round stages in the center of the audience. Such cases are isolated. In the majority of cases we have theatrical, open or some other type of stage. Further down, I will introduce you to the split of the stage spacewise. All concepts here will be relative, as we must know that the audience looks at the stage and we look at the audience. This leads to a certain misunderstanding on what is left and right—this is why we make it clear that we are looking at the audience from the stage.

This will be the approach throughout the chapter.

We assume that the stage is rectangular (Fig. 1) and is split in three parts—central (middle), left and right (Fig. 2). Another way to split the stage may be front, middle and back (Fig. 3). Besides, there are front left, front right and front central parts, plus back left, back right and back central parts (Fig. 4).

Thus we come to mention the proscenium or fore-stage. What is the proscenium? This is a Latinized word from Greek which means in front of the stage. In the theatre, proscenium is the name given to the front part of the stage before the curtain.

The forms of the proscenium may vary: arched, trapezium-shaped, a walk platform leading to the midst of the audience, or there may be two walks of different directions and length. There are no limitations. It all depends on the goals and tasks set by the producer. Specially constructed proscenia are not present everywhere. But the concept is present on every stage.

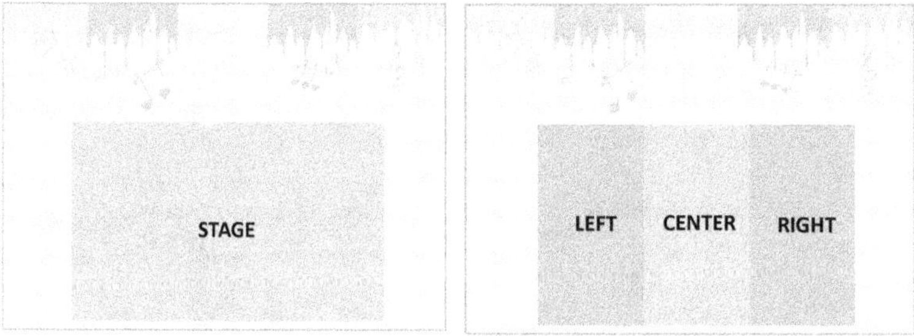

Figure 1 **Figure 2**

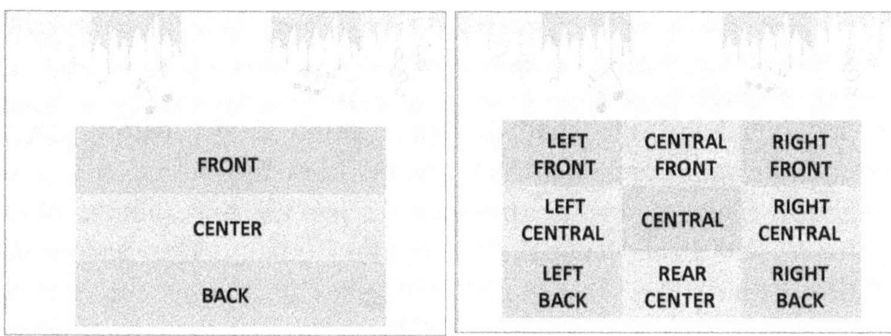

Figure 3 **Figure 4**

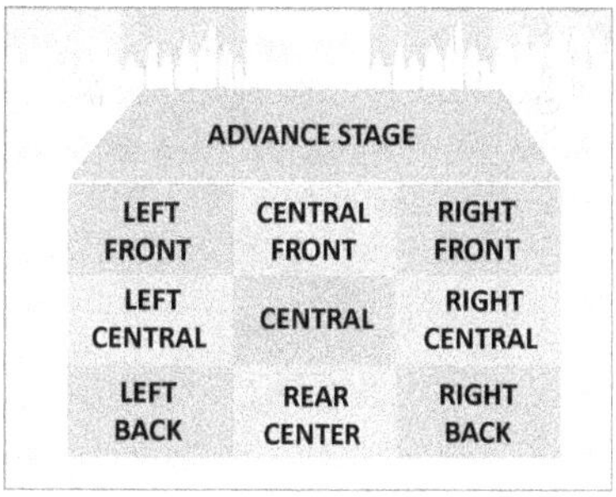

ADVANCE STAGE
LEFT FRONT CENTRAL FRONT RIGHT FRONT
LEFT CENTRAL CENTRAL RIGHT CENTRAL
LEFT BACK REAR CENTER RIGHT BACK

Figure 5

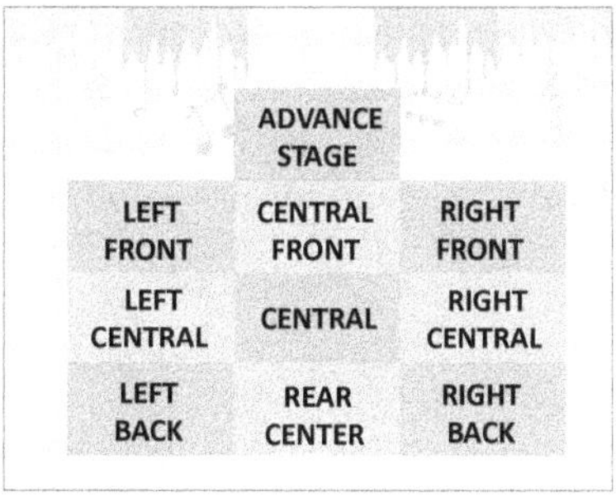

ADVANCE STAGE
LEFT FRONT CENTRAL FRONT RIGHT FRONT
LEFT CENTRAL CENTRAL RIGHT CENTRAL
LEFT BACK REAR CENTER RIGHT BACK

Figure 6

The following illustrations (Figs. 7 and 8) show how the sound monitors are placed—they provide us with feedback for the end sound—the one which goes to the audience. Here we need to emphasize that the sound director has tuned the system so the performer can hear the best sound in the central stage part as well as in some special places. As shown in the illustrations, the monitor order may be arched, thus parallel to the scene, or rectangular—surrounding a zone defined by the producer and the sound engineer.

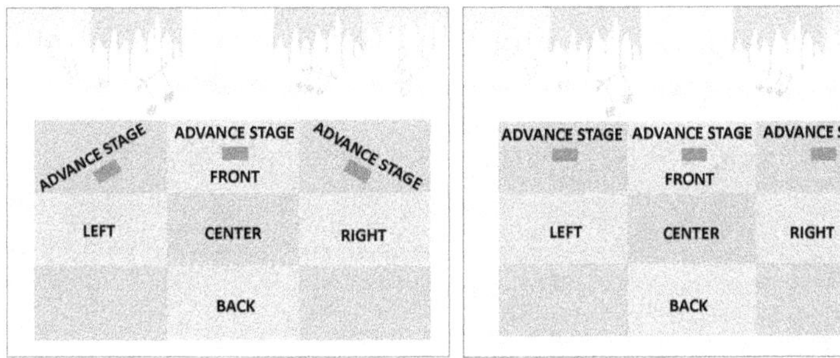

Figure 7 **Figure 8**

We need to note that the proscenium is the whole space behind the monitors on the stage and is in the direction of the audience. This is easily understandable—we are talking of a platform where we have the best sound quality. This particular platform limits the stage space, but gives us the specific space, which is our stage. I repeat, everything behind the monitors is our *proscenium*. How do we perform if there are no monitors on the stage and we use the so-called "in-ear" monitors? That is, we have earphones to get the sound back. In this case the proscenium will be behind the level of the loudspeakers, set for the sound installation equipment and/or outside of the general light arrangements prepared by the lighting engineers (Fig. 9).

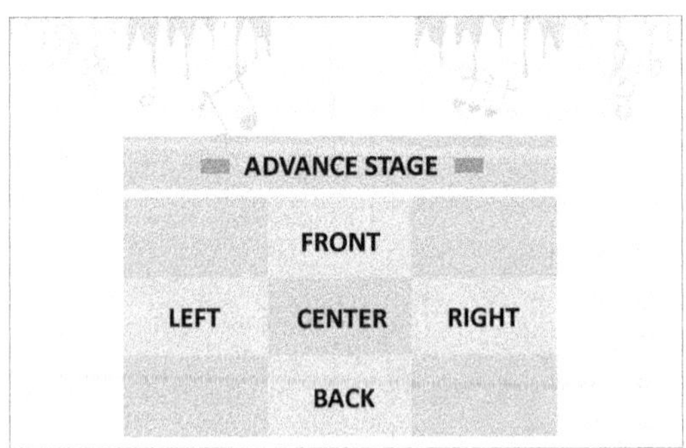

Figure 9

Everything outside the described zone and directed at the audience is the proscenium.

It is now time to pay attention to the audience. How is the audience split in the space? Again we have in mind the physical aspect and how we look at it—from the stage.

I will dwell on the simplest variant as that is what concerns us in practice. From the angle of the actor, the audience is split in three parts—middle, left and right (Fig. 10).

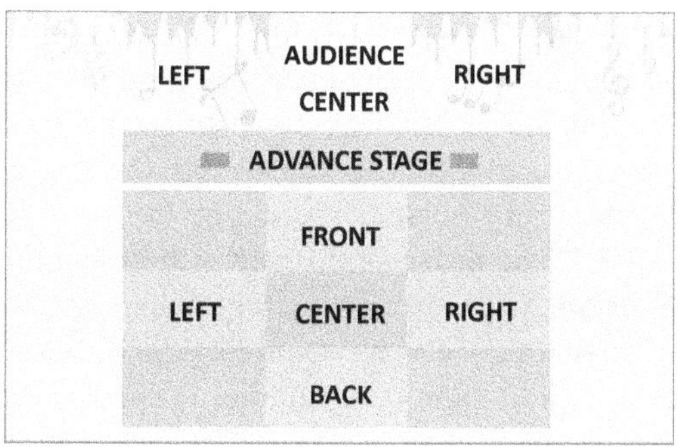

Figure 10

We do not go into too many details about the audience the way we have about the stage. Actually, the split made for the stage can be transferred onto the audience. However, this is not very important. What is more important are the cases when we have an audience at two or more levels either in the hall or in the open space where we hold our concert or participate in one.

In cases of the audience on several levels, we should know that besides the three parts just mentioned, we have the same parts but on the two or three levels. You may ask whether this is not clear sans an explanation. The answer is yes, it is easily understood, but it needs to be mentioned in order to clarify whatever may be ambiguous or doubtful from the theoretical point of view. There is one more reason: it will be useful to have looked into this variant of the audience split when the moment of practical work with the audience comes. The audience is the "interlocutor" who listens to and watches our story. They must respond to what we tell them from the stage. They need to be convinced of what we present. They will award us by applauding at the end of the performance or the concert and they must be happy to have listened to and watched us. By their reactions, they provide us with feedback on the reception to our performance.

Conclusion

Besides the technical equipment—lights and sound equipment—on the stage and around it, there may be "pockets" or "sleeves," scenography, stairs, additional platforms, screens, advertising boards and what not. The lights are situated above the stage and at times the sound equipment too. The stage is split in three parts—middle, left and right, the parts being defined as we look at the audience from the stage. The stage has a proscenium which is either specially constructed or represents the space behind the monitoring system and outside the major lit space (the comfort zone of the actor). The proscenium may also be behind the sound equipment line at the front of the stage when we have "in ear" headphones. Then there are no monitors on the stage. We split the audience into left, right and middle. A specific case is when the audience is on two or more levels. Then we split each level in the same three parts.

Chapter 3

Body Position and Communication with the Audience

In this chapter you will learn about the correct positions of the body during the performance. We will discuss the exceptions. You will be introduced to the basic rules of communication with the audience.

Communication with people, regardless whether on stage or not, involves more than only talking or singing. Dancing, facial expressions, gestures, costumes, the eyes, all these belong to our skills of conveying our message, our story to those listening or watching. Let us first talk about the basic positions of the body in the direction of the audience. The fact is that people who watch and listen to us understand body language. Though not all of them "speak" body language, this must be taken very seriously indeed when we think about the positions of the body.

The three basic positions are: face turned to the audience (Fig. 1), left shoulder turned to the audience (Fig. 2) and right shoulder turned to the audience (Fig. 3).

Stage Performance for Singers: A Practical Course in 12 Basic Steps
Martin Karnolsky

ISBN 978-981-4800-20-4 (Paperback), 978-0-429-42869-2 (eBook)
www.panstanford.com

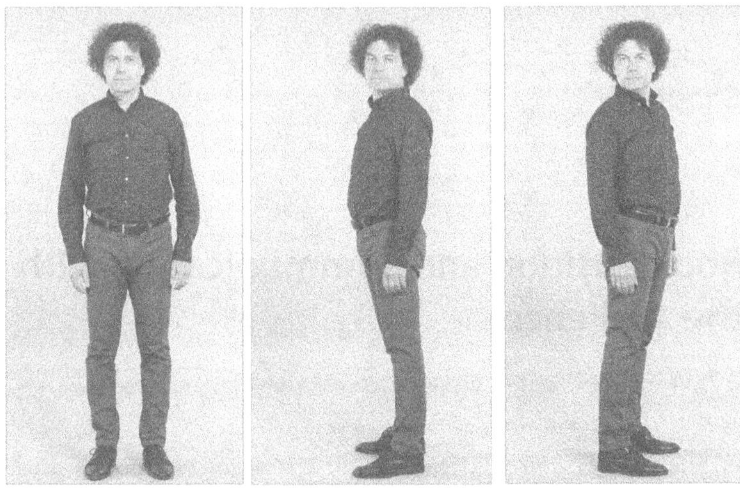

Figure 1 **Figure 2** **Figure 3**

Nothing new so far. What is not allowed or what cannot be recommended is the position with our backs turned to the audience—except for the moments of well-grounded behavior when we turn around. Or when dancing. We thus cannot avoid turning our backs to the audience altogether. However, we can take into consideration, as mentioned above, that this action is explained by our behavior. Also, it must be beautiful too.

I now return to the three "allowed" body positions. Let us look into them and analyze them. The first, with our face turned to the audience, is the one we need to analyze least of all. Still, when we face our interlocutor, the audience, we show the soft parts of the body—the belly, the neck, the groin. We can also look our "interlocutors" in the eyes. This is the shortest way to the hearts of the audience—facing them, open and looking into their eyes. Further, our hands are also visible—we will talk about them in the chapter about gestures. Whatever the case, the audience must be able to see us, we must not be hidden. This leads us to the next two positions—with our left or right shoulder facing the audience. These are the positions we usually take when changing our situation on the stage. We move, turning the maximum at 90 degrees to the audience and showing our profile. Still, we keep a part of our face in a position which allows the audience to see it and we do not turn our backs to them. We use these positions to move on the stage and also to communicate with the audience.

Let us remember what we talked about in Chapter 1. When does the performance begin? It begins while we are still backstage. We go into character. We tune up to the performance. When the moment arrives to go on stage, we head to the stage center (Fig. 4).

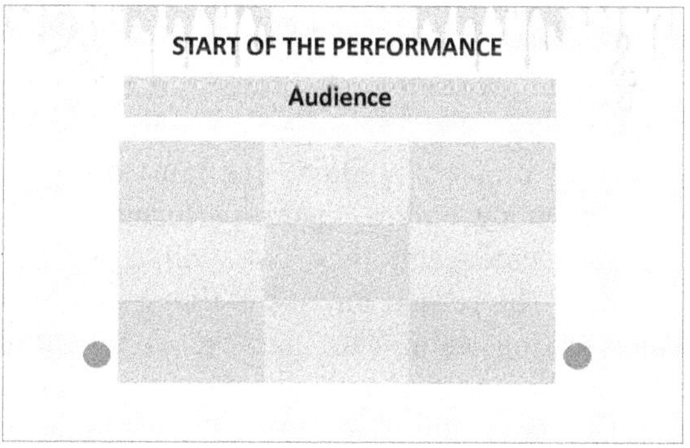

Figure 4

Of course, we can start singing with the first step on stage. We may do it backstage provided this is well grounded by the actions to follow on the stage. We can simply walk out until we reach the place we want or where the microphone on the stand is and start singing there. There are multiple variants. But we always try to reach the central part of the stage. Irrespective of whether this is the back, middle or front central part (Fig. 5).

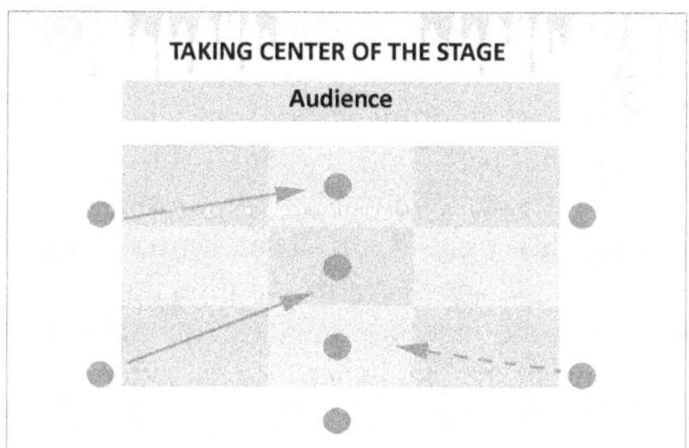

Figure 5

The idea is that our performance starts and finishes in the central part of the stage. The exceptions are:

If we start singing while going out on stage, as already mentioned.

If there is some special choreography and everything conforms to it.

The idea is to start and end in the central part of the stage.

There will be exceptions when we start singing when stepping out on stage, as mentioned above.

There may be some special choreography and everything is coordinated with it. If the choreographer has positioned us in some stage corner or on a podium, this must be well grounded and clear to everybody. Following the performance, we move to the front of the center and bow (we will cover bowing in a separate chapter). The reason for this is that by taking a position in the center the singer-and-actor declares he is "the master" of the stage. I refer you to the assertion that the audience cannot speak body language, but *understands* body language. Every person does. It includes not only behavior, gestures and facial expressions, but also the positioning in space (Allan Pease and Alan Garner, *Body Language. Talk Language*).

Assume that the beginning is over. In some way or another we have reached the central part of the stage. Now remember Chapter 2 where we discussed the split of the stage and the audience. Both the audience and the stage are split in three parts each. Having sung the first couplet, and maybe the refrain too, we need to start paying attention to the people sitting in the left and right parts of the hall.

There may be different ways of doing that. As you can see on the following illustration (Fig. 6), it is possible that we start walking from the bottom of the stage (from the back central part) to a left or right front part. By doing that, while still in the process of moving, the singer communicates with the audience before him. If he has begun his song at the front central stage part, then positioning one of his shoulders in the direction of the audience, slightly open to it, he makes a step, two or more to the left or the right section of the audience. He communicates with the spectators. By "communicating" I mean he sings specifically to this part of the audience. I also mean looks, gestures, mise-en-scene, and so forth.

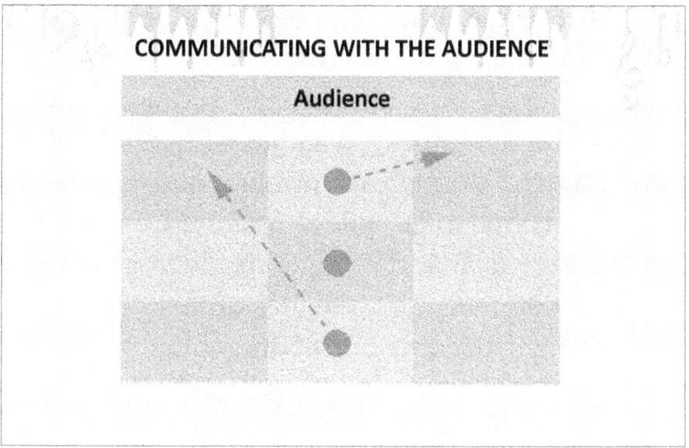

Figure 6

Having sung a couplet or a refrain or both to this part of the audience, the performer must pay attention to the section of the house at the opposite side of the hall. This may be done by singing in their direction with the very first step. It is alright to walk in front of the central part of the spectators (Fig. 7). A rule we mentioned is valid for this situation as well—it must be clear to everybody what is being done and why. There is also the other rule—i.e., we have started moving to one of the side parts of the audience from the bottom of the stage.

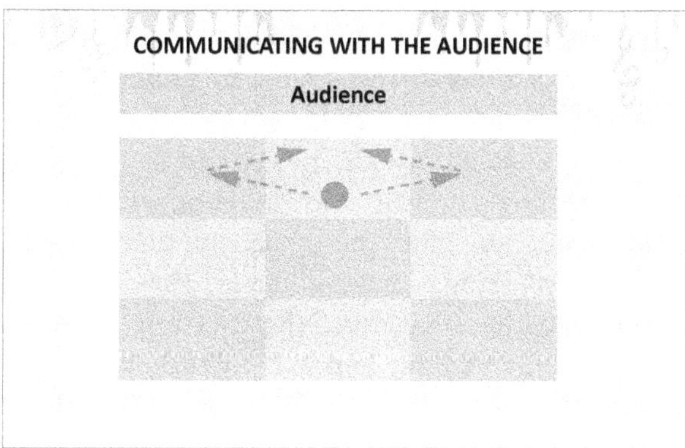

Figure 7

Having closed communicating with that part of the audience, we should go back to the center of the stage. If done for a reason, we may go again to the other side of the stage. It all depends on the context of the song, on the character we create, on the time we have for performing. A song may be two and a half minutes long, but it also may be longer, say 8 minutes. Everything is relative. It has to be thought through in advance and be well-grounded. No improvising on the stage unless prepared beforehand! At the end when the song finishes, the singer needs to head to the center. Most often I recommend that the performer comes as close as possible to the front in the direction of the audience. Thus we shorten the distance. Besides, constantly moving close to the audience shows we are not afraid of them. It shows we are looking for contact. It shows that we communicate with them. It shows that the audience is our partner in communication, in the dialogue.

Now we are back in the center. The song is over. What comes next? It is the gratitude to the spectators which we express with a bow. Another chapter is dedicated to the bow, so there is no need to deal with it now. We simply have to step out of the stage.

Stepping out must also be beautiful and in character. In the very first chapter we spoke about the actor staying in character until he or she leaves the stage. Until the actor hides backstage or leaves the stage in case it is an open or a movable one. To render that beautifully we rely not only on our preparation, but also on our good character and upbringing and sense of proportion. Remember the many occasions you have seen actors imitating a bow with a quick movement and then even more rapidly disappear from the stage? I call this disrespect to the audience. Our goodbye to the audience is as important as our appearance on stage. Besides mastering the bow as an artistic means and as part of the song, we need to learn how to "hear" the audience, so that stepping off the stage becomes beautiful. The applause helps us get oriented on a great many things. Having made our sufficiently long, respectful bow to the spectators, there is one more important aspect to consider. I remind you not to turn your back to the audience. And thus we come to these exceptions when we have the opportunity to "show" our backs.

If the exit is at the rear of the stage, this means that, willy-nilly, we will show our backs to the audience. Walking backwards trying not to show our backs will not be more beautiful or comfortable. And it is more difficult. It is uglier. It is also dangerous as we may slip and fall on the stage. What do we do then? We take a step or two back, then turn around in order to make a graceful exit. If the audience wishes so and applauds, we can make several bows while stepping backwards. Then we take one more step backwards, turn and leave the stage. If the exit is at the level of the front of the stage, the case becomes different. There is no need to take those steps back. Having bowed, we simply turn to the exit and leave. This is natural. At first, all the above sounds logical and understandable. However, when the performer steps on the stage, he may forget a great many things. Stress has a way of making one forget things that have not turned into habit as a result of good preparation. To emphasize this: under stress one turns back to old habits. And if there is no practice of correct positioning on the stage, of correct communication with the audience, what would the actor and singer return to? The answer is: to what he knows best. The pedagogue should eliminate the need to make too many suggestions, leaving the suitable course to the discretion of only the singer. Reading these words, many may smile condescendingly. They would say that at the nascent level of stage performance, training should be a bit more rigorous. I would not agree with this approach. Here is an example: an individual's strongest apprehension stems from the fear of *talking in front of an audience.* And is singing not a form of talking in front of an audience? 74% of the world's population is afraid of talking before an audience. This fear is composed of many elements, but suffice it to say that the fear of death is far less and affects only 68% of people (http://www.statisticbrain.com/fear-phobia-statistics/—28.10.2014). We can thus conclude that each element of the preparation of the singer and actor and his general preparation are of enormous importance and practice is absolutely vital.

Conclusion

In this chapter we have clarified on some issues of body positioning. We show our profile and face the audience. In this way our face is in an always visible position. We do not stand with our backs to the audience although there are some exceptions. For good and correct communication with the audience, we try to start our performance at the center of the stage, communicate with the audience on the left and on the right and close the performance in the center. Having bowed, we take at least one step backwards and it is only then that we turn and go out if the exit is at the rear of the stage. If the exit is situated on the left or the right front part, after the bow we simply walk in its direction, turned sideways to the audience.

Chapter 4

Using the Microphone

In this chapter you will be introduced to how to hold the microphone correctly and how to conduct yourself when you move on the stage with a microphone in hand. Further, how to communicate with the audience if the microphone is on a stand and what we must *not* do with it. Plus, what this technical device is.

Before we venture into using the microphone, we need to explain what a microphone is. The microphone is a device which changes sound waves into alternating electrical current by means of a vibrating diaphragm and is used in the recording and broadcasting of speech, music, etc. The word is of Greek origin, "micro" meaning small and "phone"—voice. The meaning provides us with the natural path of thinking about how to use the microphone. It is the first link in the chain and it transmits audio information to the sound recording equipment, radio, TV, cinema, telephones and other types of equipment and communication systems. The definition of the microphone synthesizes its role in our job. The microphone is an instrument! It is not an accessory, a part of the scenography or a toy. It is our "voice." It is our instrument the way our voice is. The microphone is our best friend among all the technical equipment on the stage, as all the rest depends on the human factor in the technical personnel, including switching them on "centrally." But if we have the ideal

Stage Performance for Singers: A Practical Course in 12 Basic Steps
Martin Karnolsky

ISBN 978-981-4800-20-4 (Paperback), 978-0-429-42869-2 (eBook)
www.panstanford.com

technical conditions and if we exclude them as a factor in our performance, the microphone is our instrument. We need to master it to perfection! It must not hinder us or be an unwitting adversary during the performance.

Types of microphones: there are two kinds by way of transmitting the audio information to the equipment for distribution: via a conductor (Fig. 1) and via a radio transmitter and a radio receiver (Fig. 2). We need to mention here two more variants of the so-called radio microphones. One is the classical which looks like the usual cord microphone (Fig. 3). The other is the head set—the microphone which is fixed on the head (Fig. 4). In this case we can use both our hands in the course of the performance as we do not need to hold it. Again, we have two variants. With the first one the "head" of the microphone is positioned in front of the mouth of the person talking or singing. The second one uses another technology and is fixed on the forehead or elsewhere on the head of the performer. The color is usually that of the body and it is not easily visible, in particular, from afar.

These microphones are often used in opera, musical comedy and chamber music. Actually, the mikes are used whenever the costume does not suppose a microphone of any type to be put in front of the face of the performer. There is one more way to use a mike in a situation in which it must not be visible. This system is still in use, though somewhat outdated. The variant is the microphone hung above the stage. These are used for recording, as also during classical and chamber concerts and opera and musical comedy spectacles when they serve the sound distribution in the hall.

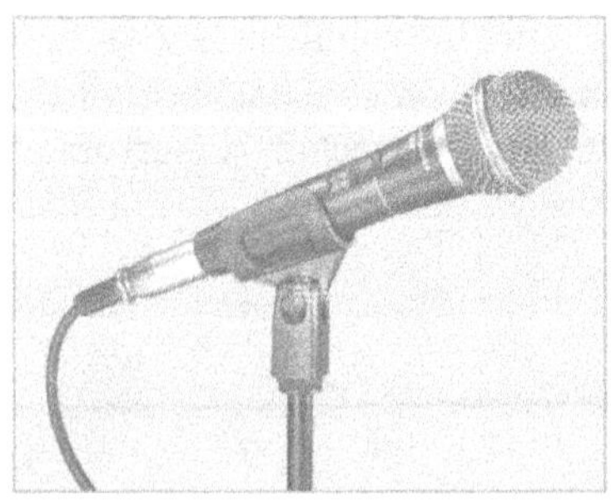

Figure 1

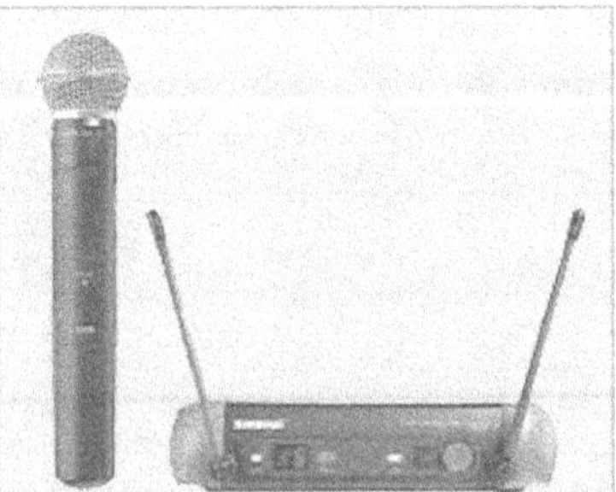

Figure 2

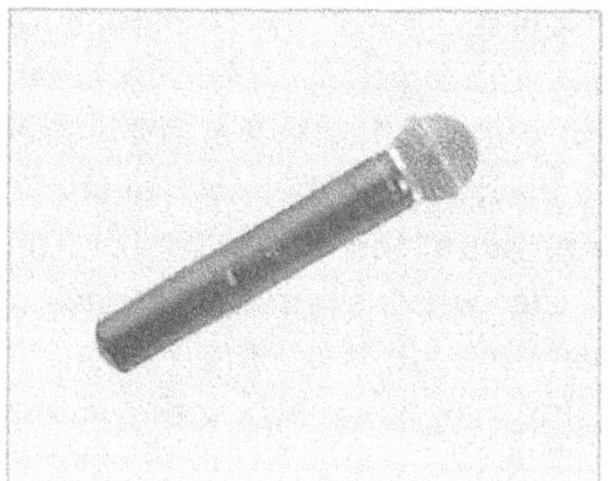

Figure 3

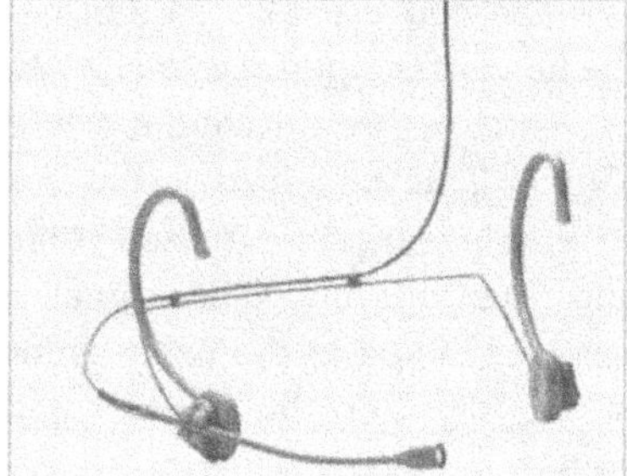

Figure 4

Let us return to the major subject of Chapter 4. Why is it important to know the mechanism? Because this knowledge is of vital importance to our success. Though the technical aspects are not our concern, it would be useful to mention the several types of microphones: dynamic, condenser, carbon and ribbon. The two most used microphones are dynamic (Fig. 5) and condenser (Fig. 6). Without getting into too many technical details, we need to know that the microphone has a "head," a body, a cord or antenna and possibly, a receiver. The "head" hides the membrane (the diaphragm) which receives the sound waves we produce. It transmits these sound waves to an electromagnet or a condenser. In the case of the headset microphone, the body is in a separate box to which the sound from the head or the membrane is sent via a wire. The transformed sound is then transmitted to a radio transmitter. Further, via the antenna the sound reaches the receiver which is part of the sound equipment.

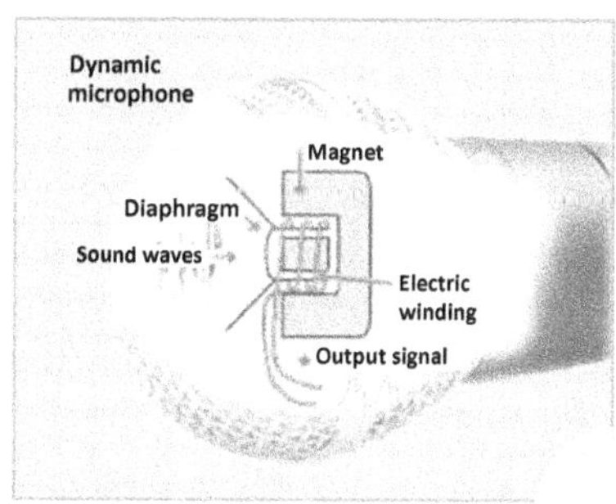

Figure 5

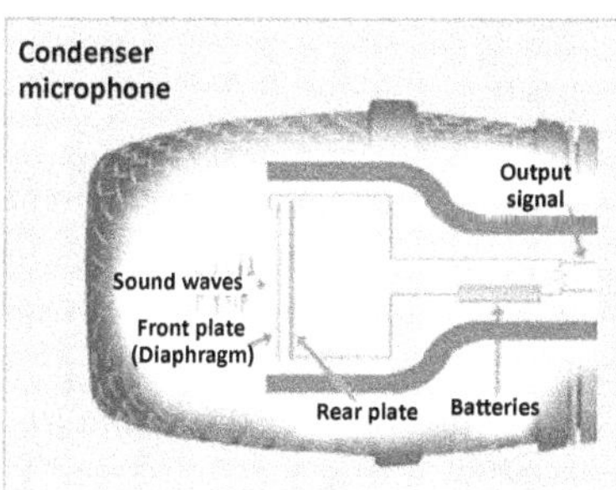

Figure 6

The above is also true of headsets or "fixed" microphones for the head of the performer (Fig. 7a).

In case the microphone has no wire and it is not a headset (Fig. 7b), all the above occurs in the body where the electromagnet or condenser are situated, together with the radio transmitter and the antenna. The signal of the wireless mike reaches a receiver linked to the basic sound equipment. If the microphone is wired (Fig. 7c), the transformed audio signal reaches the sound equipment via the wire.

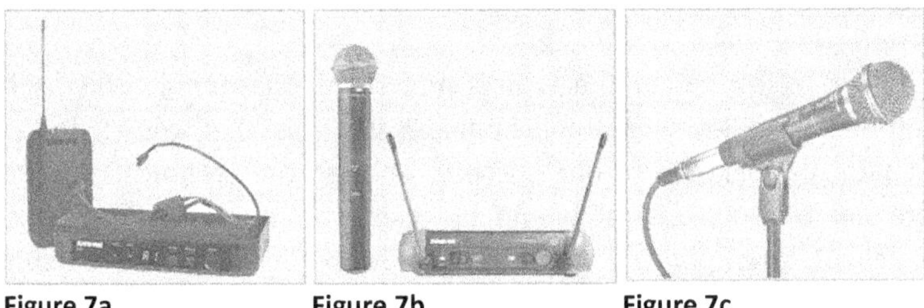

Figure 7a **Figure 7b** **Figure 7c**

In form and appearance mikes can be various. They may have a modern design, may be retro, big or small. This is not of interest to us as they all basically do the same job—they transmit our voice to the sound equipment and from there to the audience (Fig. 8).

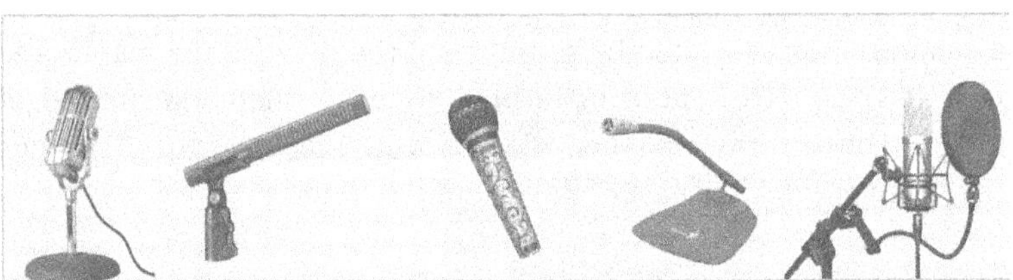

Figure 8

We need to add that when holding the microphone our hands may be put in the correct or wrong positions. In all cases when we talk about holding the microphone, it is the hand which is the mike "stand" and its position vis-a-vis the position of the actor must not vary. Namely: we hold the mike at several centimeters from the mouth, slightly lower and at an angle of approximately 45 degrees to the face of the performer. The aim is not to hide the face (Fig. 9).

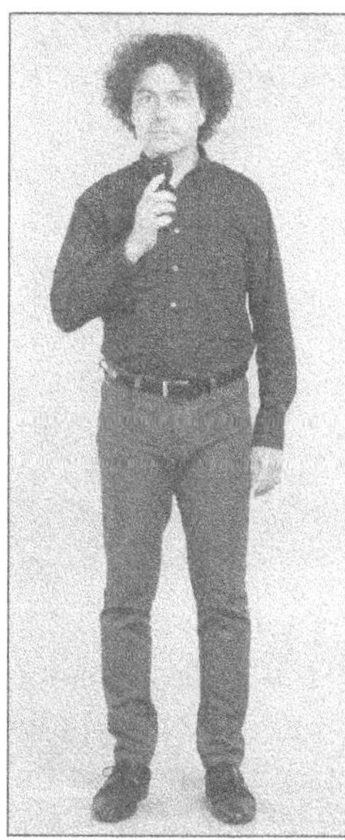
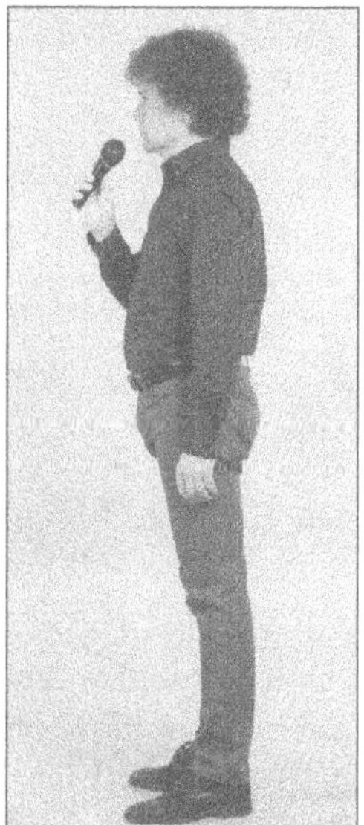
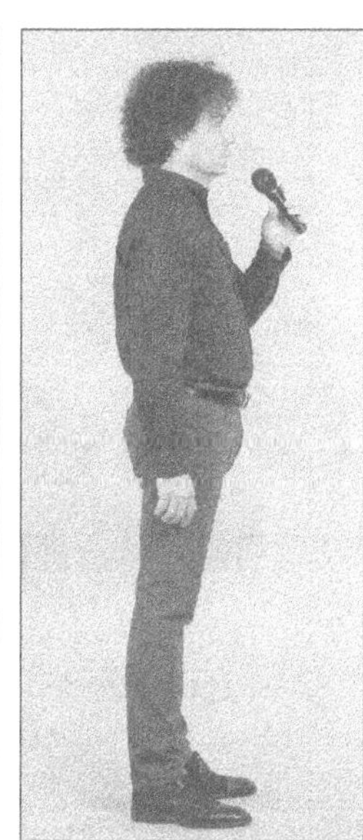

Figure 9

We must not hide behind the microphone. We hold it by the body and not by the head. This allows the sound to "live" acoustically in space in a natural way. Covering the head of the microphone often causes microphone effects. The sound could even change to that of a telephone receiver and no sound engineer can bring the sound back to the one of the performer. We hold the microphone in one hand. Holding it in two hands for a long time only means that we do not know what to do with the free hand! As an exception we can do that for some fleeting moments meant to enhance the role, show a plea or something else—but only for a few seconds! We will return to this aspect when we talk about gestures, but I would like to stress that a microphone held by two hands with eyes closed do not make the performance more emotional for the audience (Fig. 10).

If the microphone is a handset do not move your hand in front of your mouth (Fig. 11). People may think you are not ready to do anything with your hands while singing and hence you are looking for a place to put them and keep them busy. Once set, this microphone should not be touched, except for some positional corrections! Use your hands for gesturing.

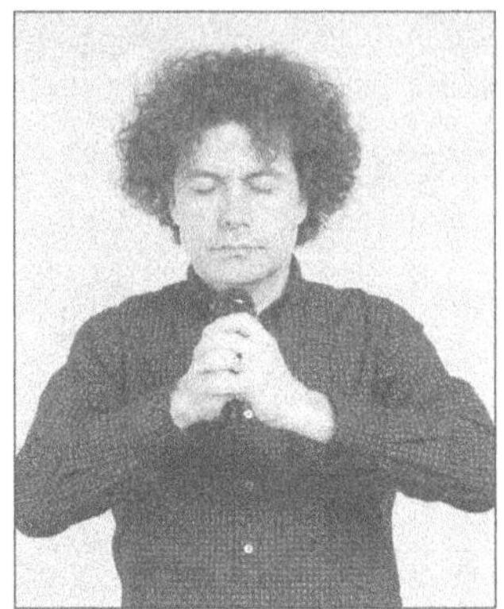
Figure 10

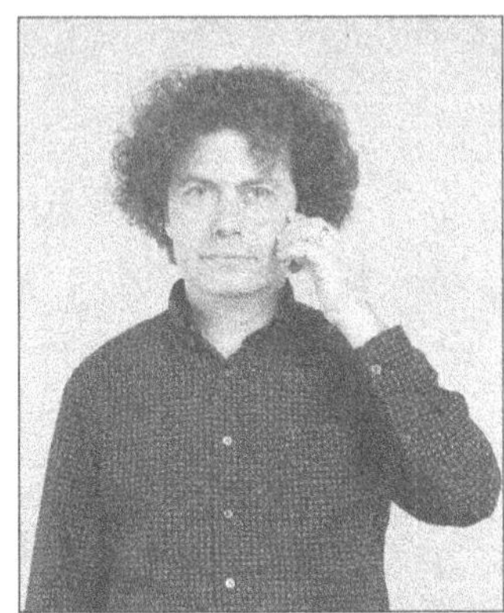
Figure 11

As I mentioned, the hand which holds the microphone is its stand. But what if the mike is fixed on a stand—what do we do? Just leave it be (Fig. 12). So far it has not fallen and it is not likely to fall now. Do not hold it! Do not hold the stand! And never with both your hands (Fig. 13)! On the contrary—if you touch it, it may fall. As usual, there may be exceptions again. You can get hold of the microphone or of the stand if you sort of touch the character, or in case of something which will give a grounding to the action (Fig. 14). But never touch the stand if you have taken the mike off it except if you need to move it or perform some other legitimate action with it.

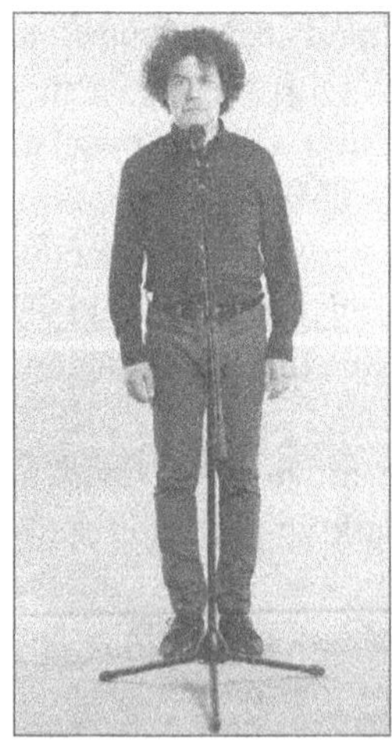
Figure 12

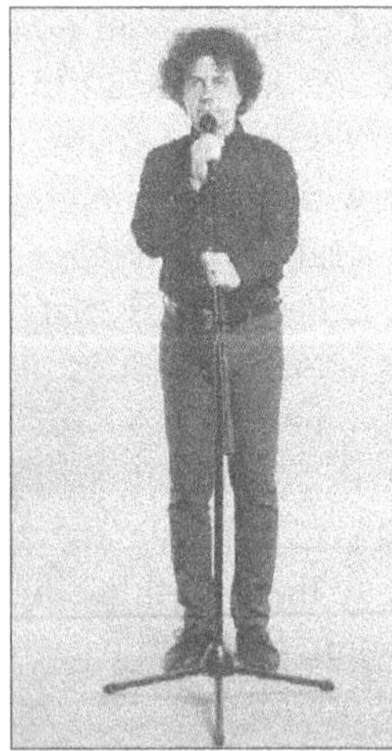
Figure 13

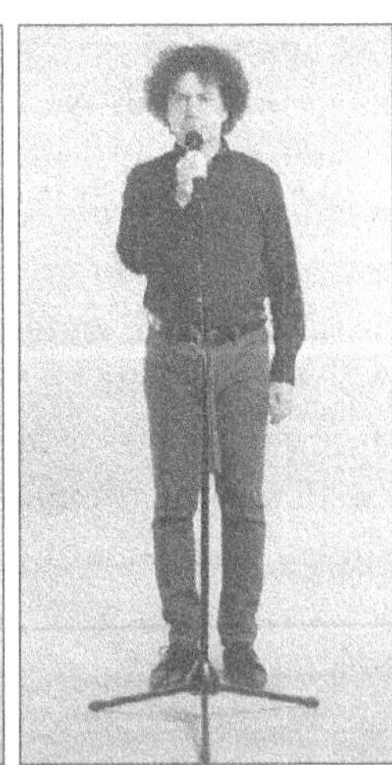
Figure 14

We need to mention that there may be exceptions when using the microphone and working with it. One is the culture of rap which has imposed a very different approach to the use of the microphone. It is something of a success symbol like the smoking of a cigar. The mike is held in front of the face with its back part held high. Of course, the face is hidden, but this is considered to be the norm with this style (Fig. 15).

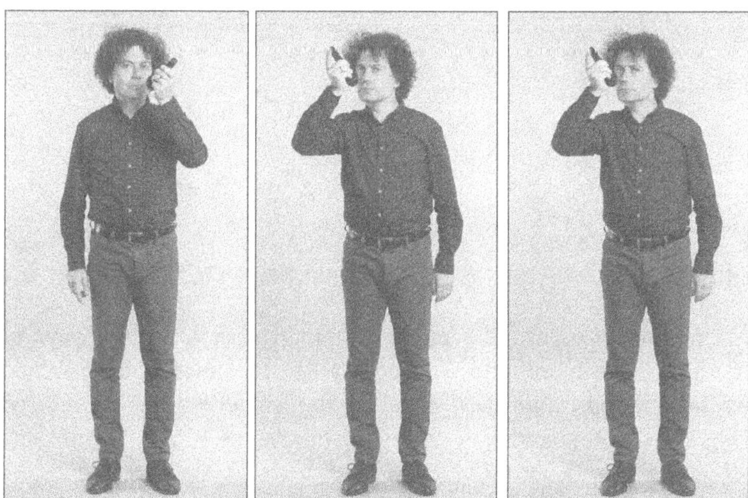

Figure 15

The beat box performers *must* hold the microphone by the head in spite of the danger of the microphonic effect. Such performers aim at sound distortion. They use their instrument in a manner slightly different than the usual. They use the whole spectrum of sounds which the mike can produce, irrespective of whether it is parasitic or not regarding the singing (Fig. 16).

Let us examine the exceptions with other singing styles. In rock music there is an image which is emblematic—that of Freddie Mercury—and nobody can mistake him. He has his registered brand. He takes the upper part of the stand together with the microphone and uses it. Is this wrong? I think it is a mistake which has developed into a brand and is no longer a mistake but a behavioral pattern. He also holds the stand and carries or bends it (Fig. 17).

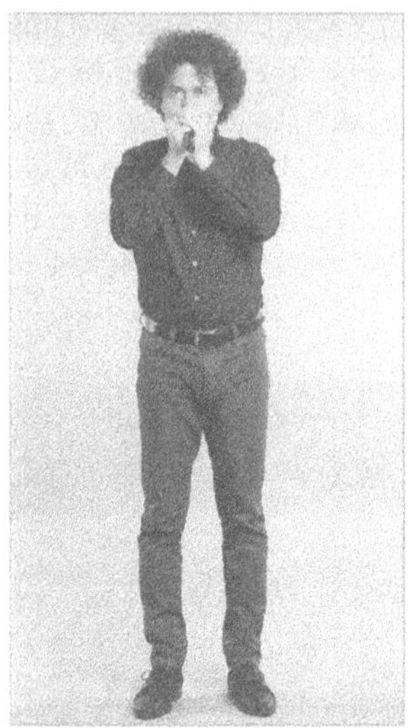

Figure 16

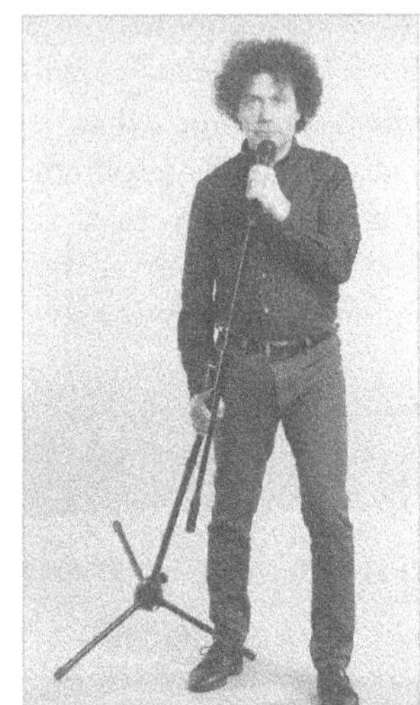

Figure 17

Let us look into the parasitic and not so beautiful ways of holding the microphone. To begin with, the microphone is held by both hands and (God forbid!) the singer's eyes are closed (Fig. 18).

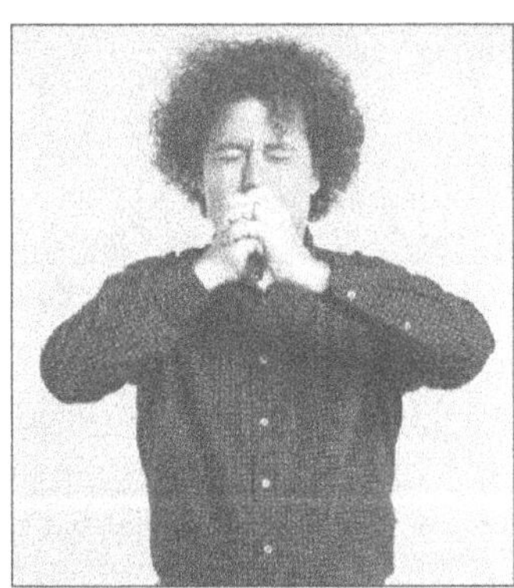

Figure 18

Or the microphone is on the stand, held by both hands, lest it fall (Fig. 19).

A headset microphone held by one hand—I wonder why! No explanation (Fig. 20).

The microphone to be held by the "head" is very common—probably making the performer feel very professional (Fig. 21)?

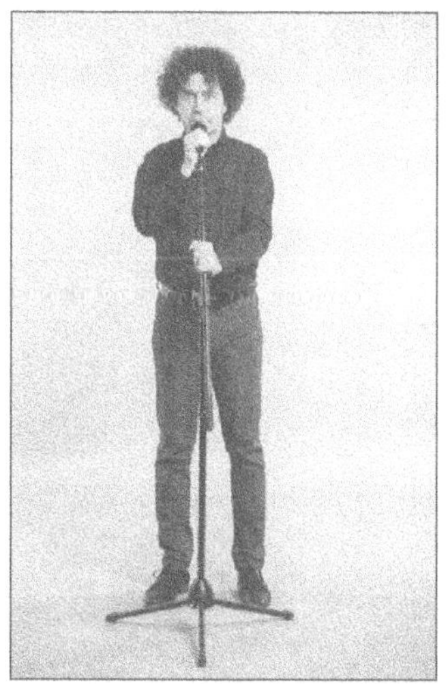

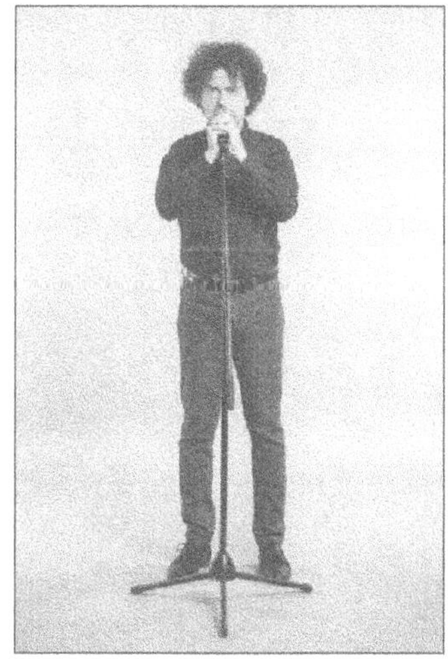

Figure 19

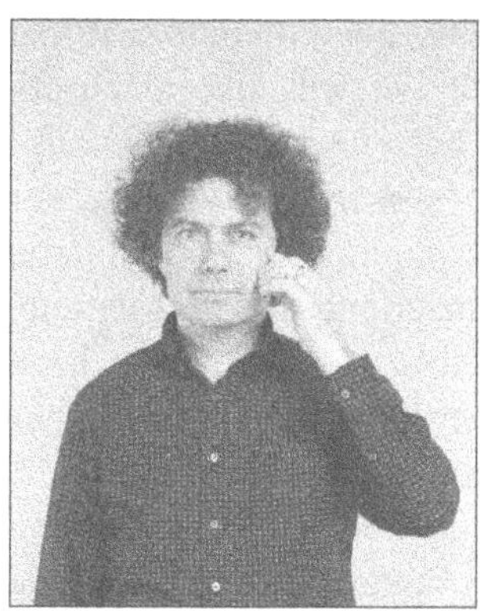

Figure 20

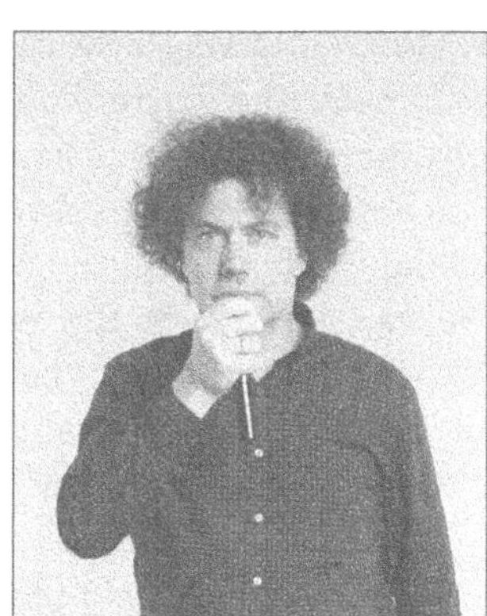

Figure 21

Holding the microphone with the thumb in front of the membrane of the "head." This position of the hand hinders the transmission of the pure sound information to the membrane (Fig. 22). The "head" will transmit a distorted or inadequately low sound to the equipment and further—to the spectators or listeners.

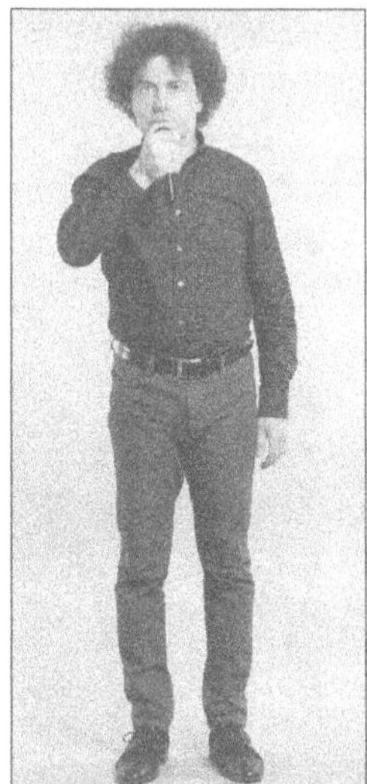
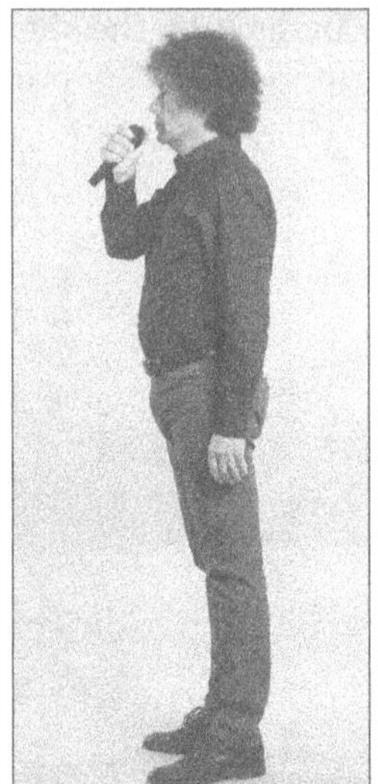
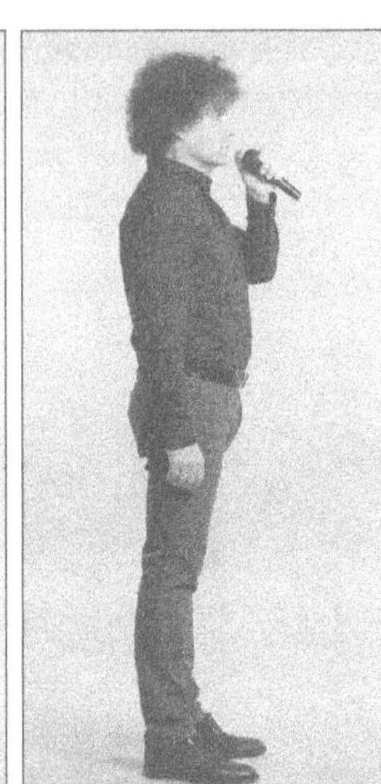

Figure 22

In the following pages when we talk about gestures, looks and other factors of communication we will elaborate on the reason not to sing with closed eyes. At this stage I would just like to repeat: the microphone will not fall! We will also elaborate on other aspects which have hitherto not been dealt with in detail.

Referring to the previous chapter—we were talking about communicating with the audience. While holding the microphone we can walk over the whole stage, including the proscenium. We can jump among the audience. Is this necessary? We have the freedom to go as far as the length of the cord will let us, or even further when there is no cord with the radio microphones.

Now let us look at behaviors which necessitate complying with the microphone. I refer you back to the example in which we go out on the stage and look for its central part (Fig. 23). Let us imagine we have started performing in the central front part of the stage. We hold the microphone in one hand. We sing a couplet. Or a refrain. It all depends on how long the song is. We can split it in parts (to be discussed further). So, we stand in the front and a part of it has been sung. We select a direction and move to the left. According to the principles of communication with the audience we move to stand in front of those sitting in the left part of the hall. We hold the microphone with the left hand (Fig. 24).

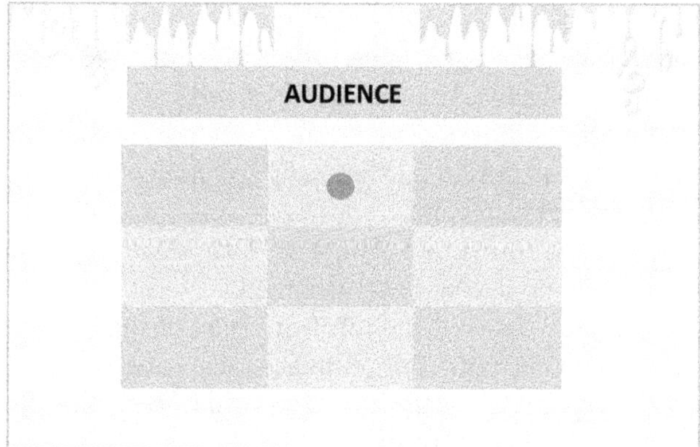

Figure 23

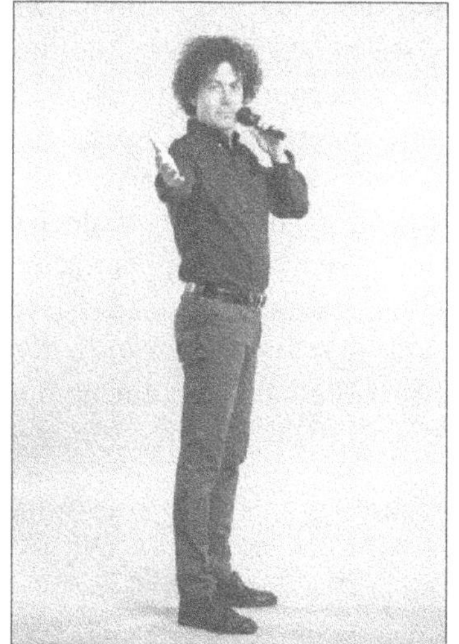

Figure 24

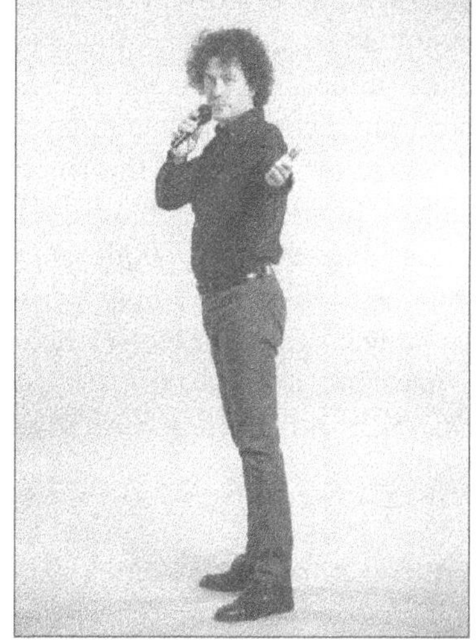

Figure 25

Do not try to remember which hand—left or right—you are holding the microphone with while you are moving. It is much easier to think that the mike is in your internal hand vis-a-vis the audience. The question, logically, is why. Because according to simple logic and to body language people accept us more easily and better when they can see the "soft" parts of our body: the belly, the groin, the neck. They are not only "soft," they are the most vulnerable body parts and we have been protecting them since the beginning of our very existence. That is, we instinctively know where we are vulnerable. When we see another person showing his vulnerable body parts to us, we feel he is not afraid of us. When we, additionally, can see his hands, we are perfectly calm (Allan Pease and Alan Garner, Body *Language. Talk Language*).

We need to convey calm to our spectators, to make them feel we do not threaten them by any means. That we are open to them. Let the audience see that we are "unarmed."

Thus we have reached the left front part of the stage and are now communicating with the audience. We have sung a second couplet or a refrain. It is time to pay attention to the people in other parts of the hall. Attention! *Attention*! We change the hand which holds the microphone during a moment when we are neither singing nor talking. That is, the right hand replaces the left during a pause. Why? There are several reasons for this. One is we may lose part of the sound quality if we move the mike. Another, more important reason is the audience becoming unfocused by our distracting movements! By movements which carry no message or additional information to what we give them with the words. Remember, people do not know why they like or dislike something, but they understand a lot of what is happening on the stage. There are things here based on upbringing; others based on body language or experience and skills to influence the audience. What is most important is not to distract the audience during our singing or talking!

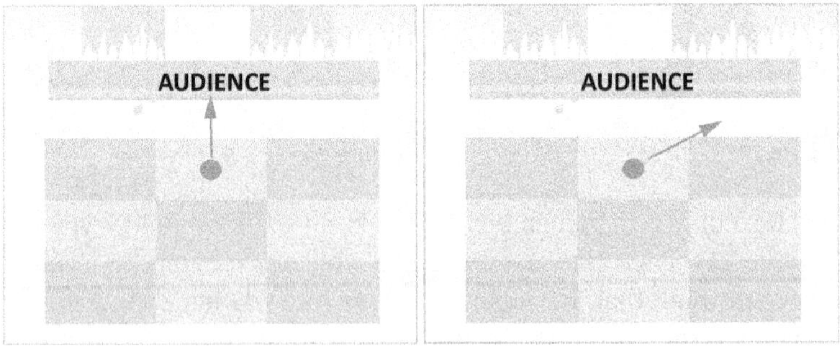

Figure 26 **Figure 27**

We have moved the microphone to our right hand which is now "internal" and we walk to the other side of the stage (Fig. 25). Do not think you must absolutely go to the other side and do it immediately at that! No. You can stop at the center and communicate with the audience in the middle of the hall (Fig. 26). Or you can communicate with the right part of the audience without reaching it (Fig. 27).

While singing to the right side of the audience, we walk in its direction. Having reached the center of the stage, we can turn and continue the "dialogue" with the central part of the audience, having communicated with the right side while moving (Figs. 28 and 29). I refer you to what has already been said. It depends on the length of the song, on the number of couplets. It depends on what role we are playing. To sum it up: there are rules, but they are not final. They may be breached and changed provided that this will be argumentative from the artistic point of view and will be beautiful. To put it in different words: we may contact the audience (Figs. 28 and 29) at the further end of the hall without going there. We may go there three times, if necessary. What is important is that this will be attractive, logical, natural and understandable to everybody. I would like to repeat one more aspect: we start the performance in the center of the stage. There is a variant in starting the performance the moment we step on stage, but we try to occupy the center. Some exceptions can happen: the choreography or a special mise-en-scene can lead us to other spots on the stage which we will not discuss now (Fig. 30). Let us not forget: having started at the center we must finish there too.

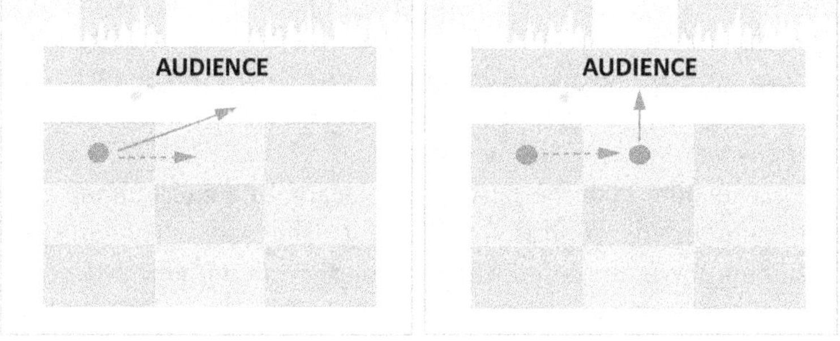

Figure 28 **Figure 29**

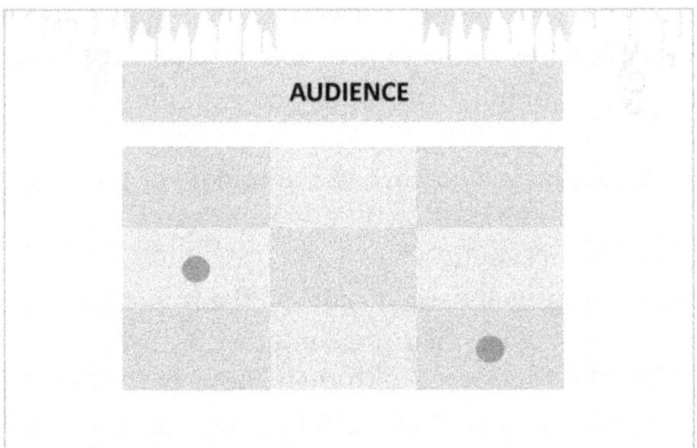

Figure 30

We need to say a few words on the position of the microphone when it is not in use. Regarding the sound equipment on the stage, we must consider the direction of the microphone during the time when we are not singing. Think about possible microphone effects. In other words, we must not point the microphone to the monitors or stand right in front of the loudspeakers which provide the sound to the hall or to some open platform. Covering the head of the microphone, as mentioned can also be dangerous because of microphonism.

We have dealt with the variants of working while holding the microphone in our hands. Now let us look into the variants in the case of a mike on a stand in the central front part, in the middle or in the rear central part. In the last two cases we can suggest taking the mike off the stand and walking forward to the audience. These are mixed options. If at the beginning the microphone has been held by hand and then put on the stand or vice versa, then it is a mixed technique, which hinders the performance somewhat. It has to be carefully thought through—what we gain and what we lose by this. However, these variants are possible.

Let us now take the first variant again. The microphone is on the stand in the central front part of the stage. The music is resounding. We are either standing by the microphone before the start of the music or slowly and majestically move in its direction if the song is a ballad. If the song is more dynamic and rapid, we may not have to convey some kingly manner. The important thing is to look natural and all our actions be well grounded.

Here we are at the microphone. We do not touch it. Neither the microphone nor the stand. It will not fall down. It has been waiting on the stage and will continue to do so for 3 or 4 more minutes. Here is the moment of truth! We stand behind it and start singing. We do not touch the microphone. We create our character. But it is all stiff and awkward as the microphone limits the communication to the audience before us, our movements are limited. We are hidden behind the mike. What do we do then? We can simply turn our heads *around* the microphone. However, while turning we must be careful that the microphone does not stand sidewise to us, thus making impossible good quality transmission of sound to the audience. In this case the sound will be lost, as the microphone has lost contact with the sound source—the mouth. Thus, with a look, with a gesture we have contacted the audience in the left or right part of the hall (Fig. 31).

After that we do the same, changing the direction. This conveys the feeling of being in command of both the audience and the stage (Fig. 32). If done at the right moment and in the right way. We will elaborate on that in the chapter dedicated to the look and how to use it. The end of the performance will be a look and words to the central part of the audience. The bow and leaving the stage follow. The mixed options add more drama, but we cannot say they bring a difference to what we have been discussing so far. If at the beginning the microphone was on the stand, and later it develops into performing with the microphone held in our hand, the case ends. The vice versa order is also important. You may put the mike on the stand, then take it off ten times—nothing of the above changes.

Let us see what will happen if we have one microphone for two or more performers. We can imagine that the movements of the two or three singers will be considerably limited. These are cases of a chorus or back vocals singing. This does not allow the performers' faces to be expressionless or "frozen." The behavior of the actors as an ensemble needs to be considered and, again, the behavior must be homogeneous and natural. There must be contact with the audience too.

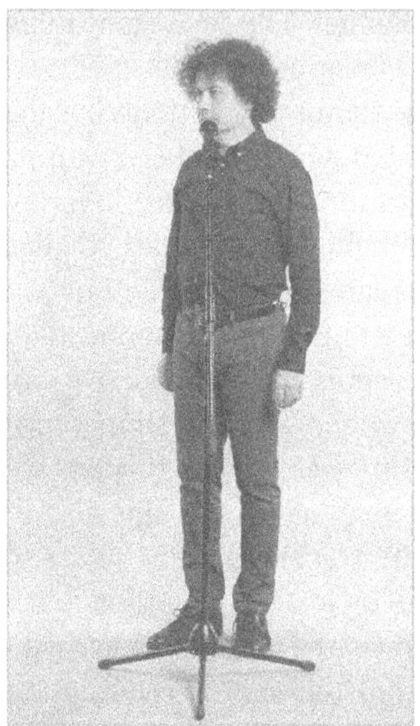

Figure 31

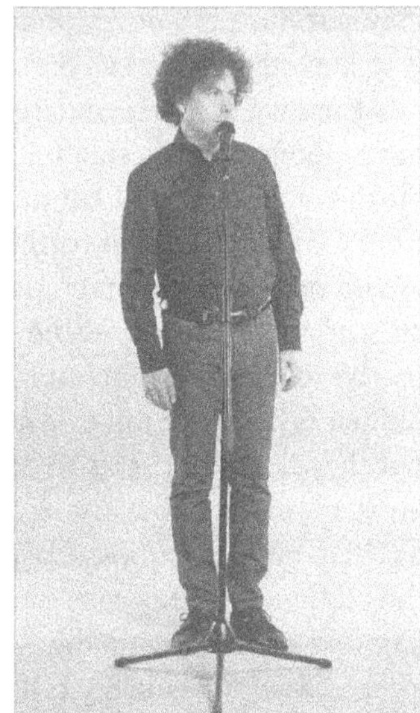

Figure 32

There are different possibilities of singing with a common microphone. Again, the above stays true. The singing will be done with the microphone on a stand or with someone holding it. Let us stress once again: the limitation of the body movements should not limit eye contact and facial expressions (Fig. 33).

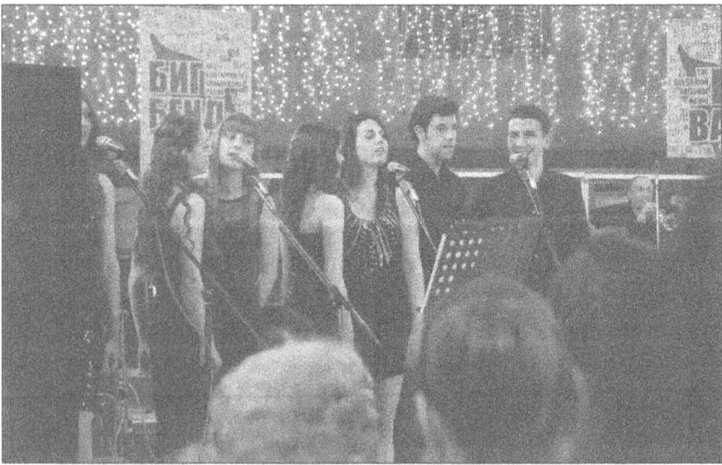

Figure 33

Entering and exiting for groups of people from the stage, their distribution and their behavior on stage is a different matter. Solo performance is the priority in everything we have said so far or will say further.

Conclusion

The microphone is a technical device which "transfers" our voice from the stage to the audience by means of transmitting the transformed electrical acoustic signal to the central sound equipment. The microphone has a head, a body and a cord or a transmitter and an antenna in the case of the radio microphone. In the latter case there is also a receiver which is in the central sound equipment. We do not hold the microphone stand or the microphone on the stand with our hands. We do not hold the microphone with both hands. We do not hold it by the head. The antenna or the back part of the microphone must point downwards so as not to cover the performer's face.

When we walk on the stage in the direction of the left or right part of the audience, we hold the microphone with the hand which is internal vis-a-vis the audience. In this way our body is open to it. We change the hand which holds the mike only when we *do not* sing. If the microphone is on the stand, we turn our heads around its head to contact the audience on the left or the right side. The rules for using the different techniques stay in force with mixed techniques. When using a common microphone because of the limited movements, the contact with the audience is established with eyes, gestures and facial expressions.

Chapter 5

Gestures

In this chapter you will learn the definitions of gestures, the phrase in the gesture, the ways to define our behavior and some of the basic positions of the hands and the body. This is one of the chapters of major importance in understanding the concept of making the body "sing."

5.1 What is a gesture? (It comes from the Latin gestus—a movement of a body part). It is a means of non-verbal communication in which by way of symbolic movements an idea or meaning is expressed. The movement is done most often by the hands and the head, but also by the body. This type of movement is called gesticulation.

Here is one more definition, perhaps a more exact one: the gesture is a movement which conveys a visual signal to the observer.

Science has proven that above 65% of human communication is *non-verbal* (by means of gestures and facial expressions) and during sexual intercourse it reaches 100% (Burgoon 1994, pp. 229–285).

We should mention that gestures have their place in the big family of arts. It is called *pantomime*, a genre of theatrical art which uses gestures and facial expressions.

Stage Performance for Singers: A Practical Course in 12 Basic Steps
Martin Karnolsky

ISBN 978-981-4800-20-4 (Paperback), 978-0-429-42869-2 (eBook)
www.panstanford.com

When talking about gestures as part of stage performance we need to add an important detail: the gesture must complement the word and not repeat it!

Examples

We all know the meaning of the words which follow: "I live in a house." There is no need to show yourself, the form of the house or how you live—how you sleep, eat, etc. Often there is no time for that. We have defined it in the context of the word to which we can add a meaning. That will be the "strong" word in the text. We will elaborate on that in the chapter about studying and working with lyrics. For now we will use the word "house."

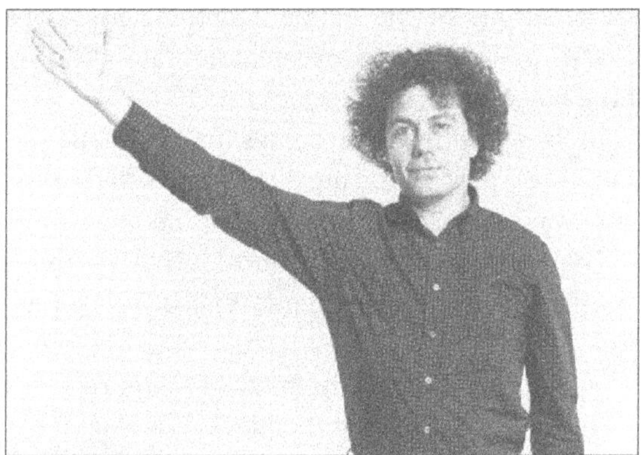

Example 1

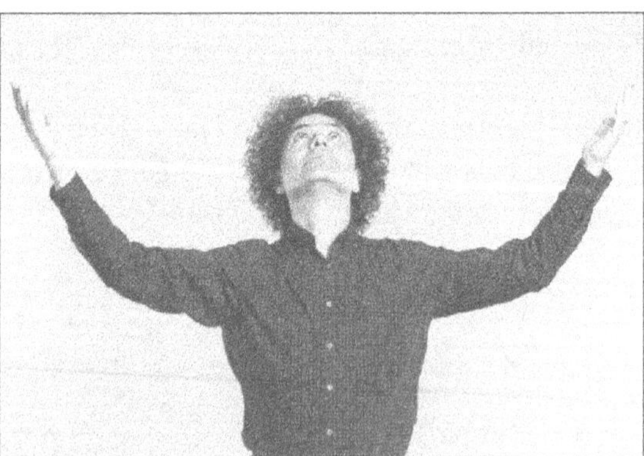

Example 2

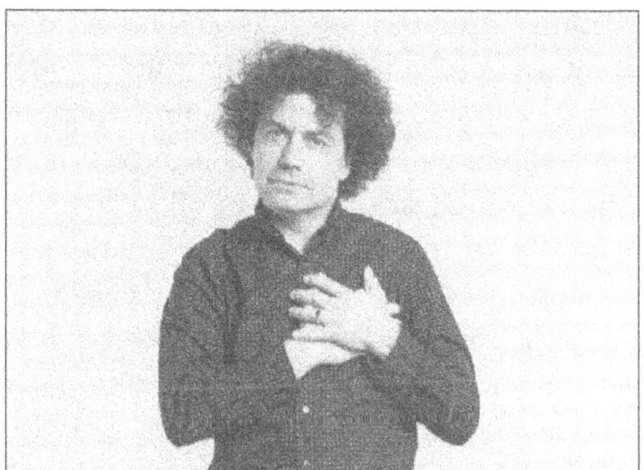

Example 3

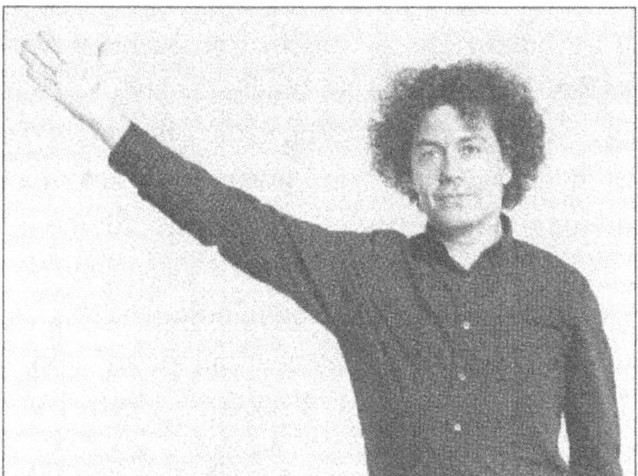

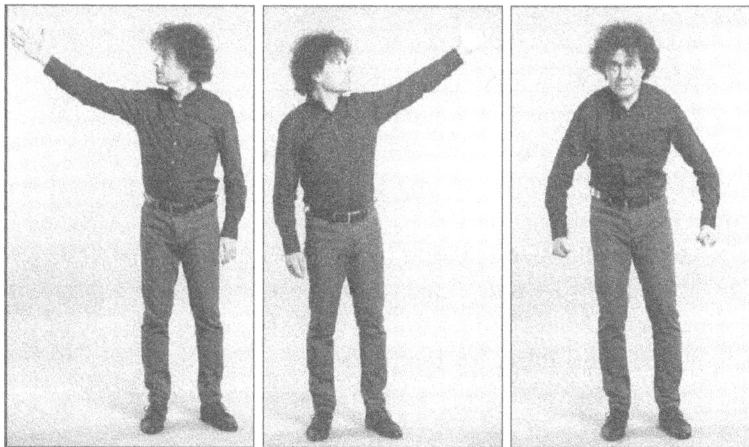

Figure 1a Figure 1b Figure 1c

Here are three examples of different types of houses. The first is far away. The second is huge, the third is our dear home. It is obvious that the same word may acquire a different meaning in the text by a single gesture. It is of no use to mention comic or parody shows which are based on the difference between gestures and words. In this way an analogy with another context of the whole message of the performance is made. That is, the gesture needs to be very carefully thought through and made in a way to reach the audience without changing its major purpose—adding more quality to the word. These are qualities which are absent in the text, but we will add them. And this is all linked to the general message of the text and our personal attitude.

Let us look at example 1—the house is far away.

"I live in a house (Fig. 1) and I often have to walk on foot to the bus stop (Fig. 1b). When I go back it is twice as hard, as I also carry the bags with purchases (Fig. 1c). It becomes clear that it is hard on us and everything is far away. It might also be boring." All that is depicted by gestures which add to the basic idea in the text.

Let us examine example 2: "I live in a house" (Fig. 2a).

"I have a terrific sports car, a small plane and a wonderful yacht (Fig. 2b). I wear expensive modern clothes and expensive jewels" (Fig. 2c).

In this example the same text develops in a different direction. Based on the text, we have already created very different circumstances. Now we project ourselves as successful people. Or we boast, if you will.

Here is example 3: "I live in a house" (Fig. 3a).

"The river of my childhood runs by it. The river of my first love (Fig. 3b). I would like my children to live here and feel the house as their own!" (Fig. 3c).

As you ca n see, this house is very different from the first two. The attitude to the house and its purpose are radically different. It is different from the point of view of the relationship with the family and the future. All that, I repeat, depends on the overall idea and purpose of the words which we will say or sing.

I would very much like to draw your attention to when and how gestures are used. First, the gesture may come before the word. Second, it may come together with it and third, it may be made after the word. There are other possibilities besides these three. There may be a gesture which will start before the specific word, continue while we pronounce it and continue after it. Or a fifth possibility—start before the word and end with it. Or even a sixth—start with the word and end after it. It will all depend on what we want to suggest to the audience. Or on what we want to add to the qualities of the word which we depict.

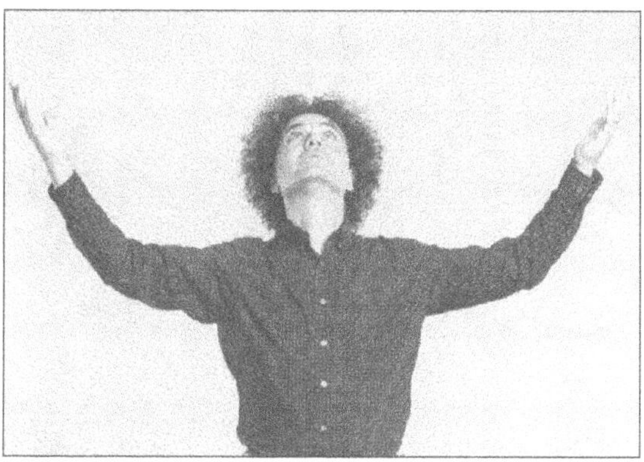

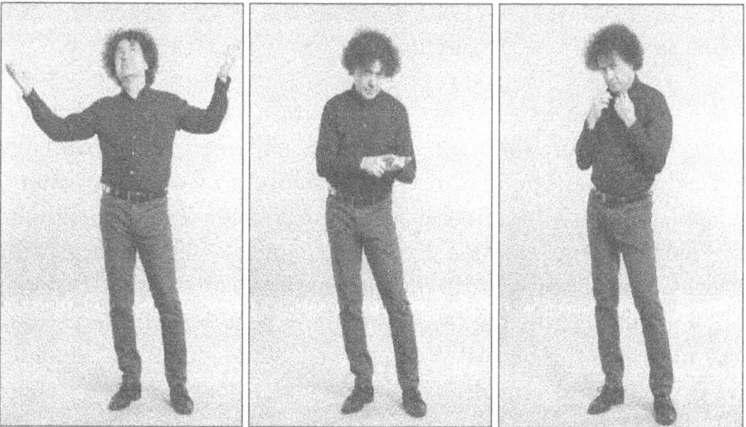

Figure 2a **Figure 2b** **Figure 2c**

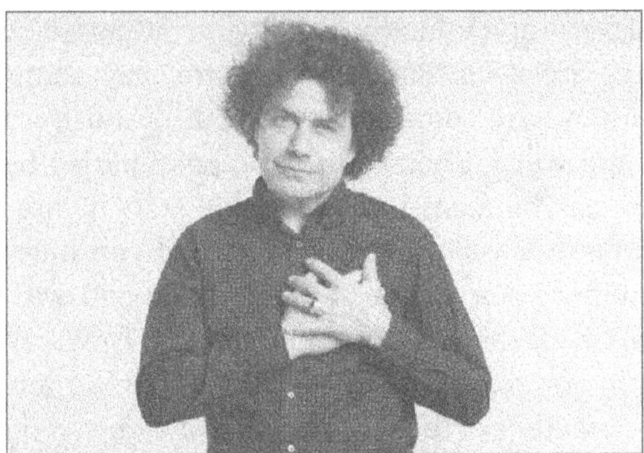

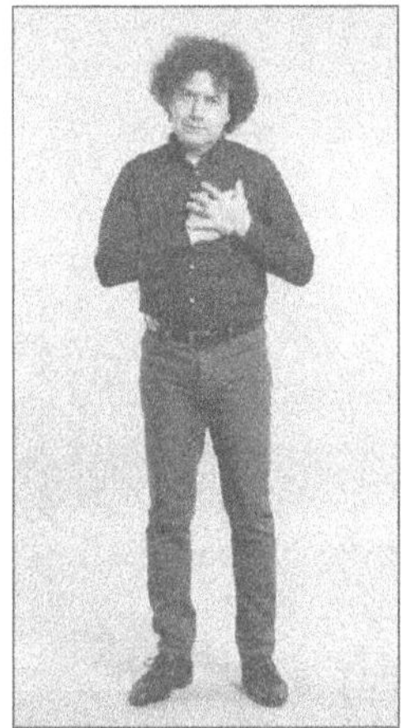

Figure 3a

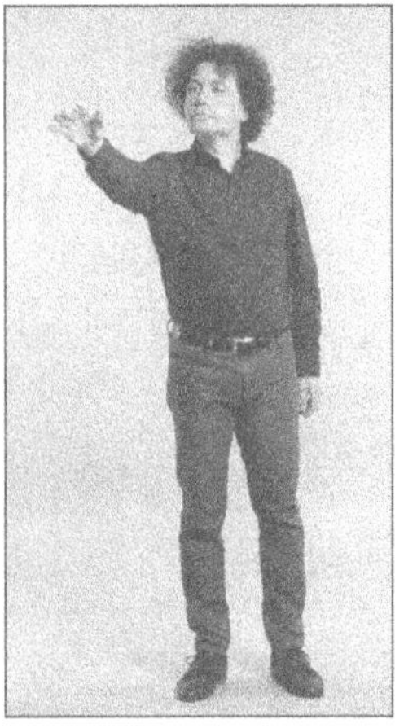

Figure 3b

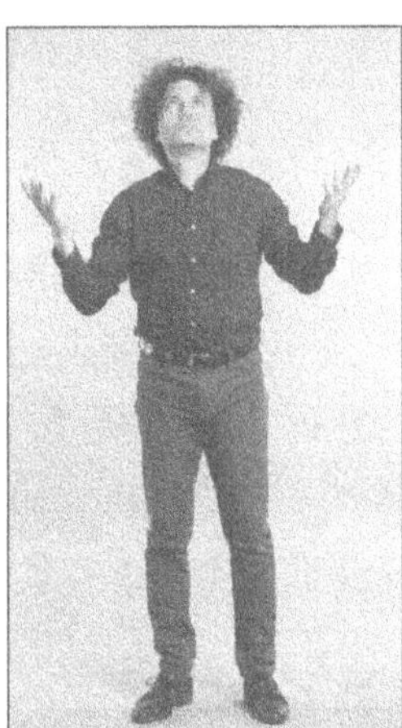

Figure 3c

5.2 Now let us see what a phrase or a sentence is. Sentences are composed of words which carry their meanings individually. From the phonetic point of view the sentence is a sequence of sounds which contains a complete piece of information, corresponding to the meaning and emotional content. Sentences are separated by pauses. Considering the phonetic characteristics, some linguists call it a phrase (from the Greek φράση—a sentence, an expression). The phrase is the biggest phonetic unit with a complete meaning. It is split into smaller phonetic units—bars and syllables. All that is linguistically fine. We can define "a phrase in the gesticulation" as a finished sequence of gestures which carry a complete meaning.

All of the variants discussed above may be examples of phrases in gesturing ("I live in a house"). Again, a chain of gestures linked to each other by their meaning and united by a specific text is called a phrase in gesticulation.

We cannot call a phrase in the gesticulation in the following:

"I live in a house" (Fig. 4a).

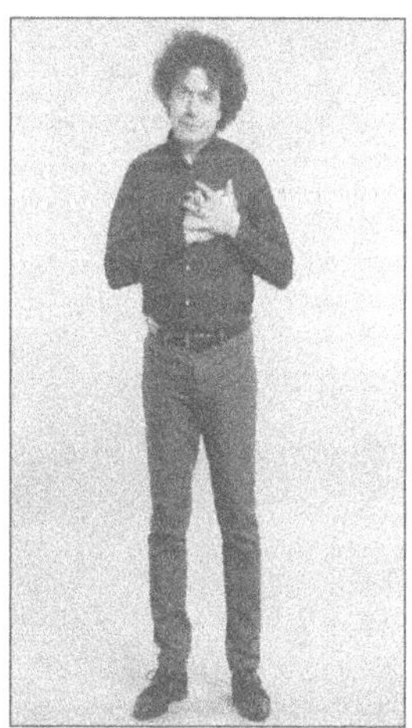

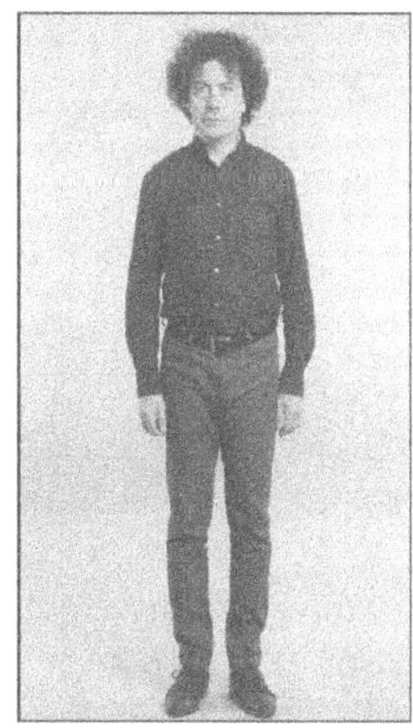

Figure 4a

"The river of my childhood runs by it" (Fig. 4b).

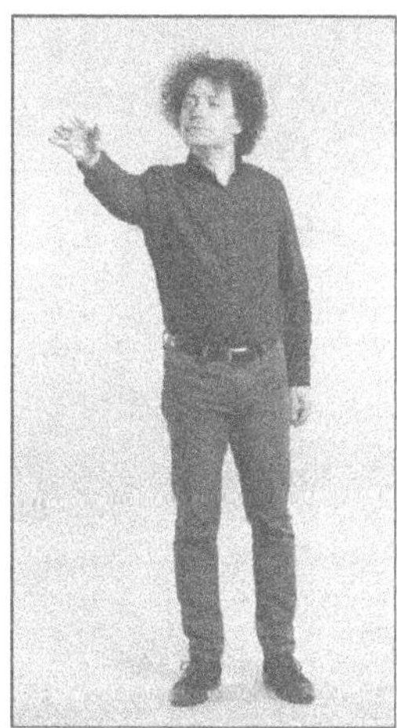

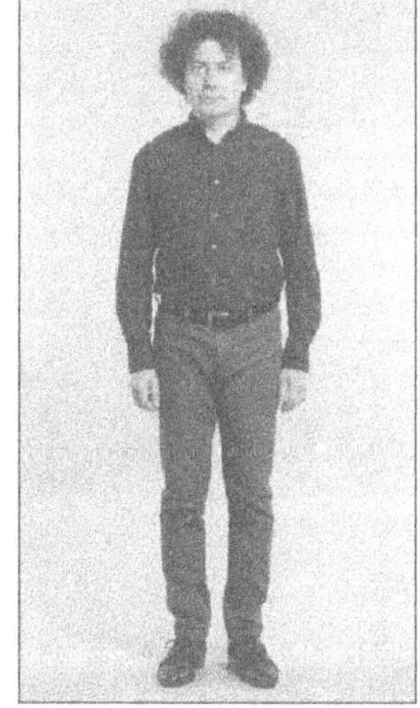

Figure 4b

"The river of my first love" (Fig. 4c).

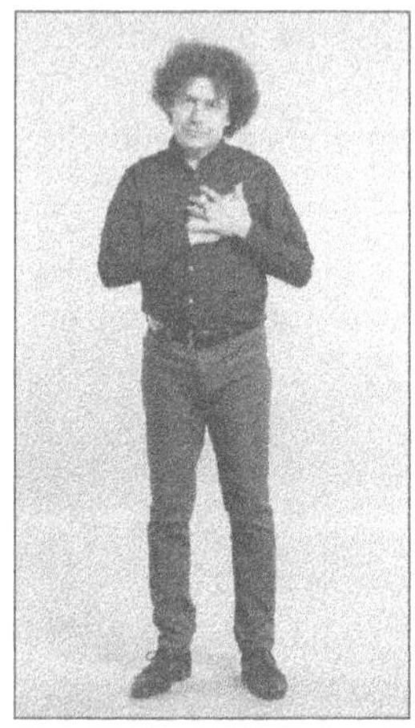
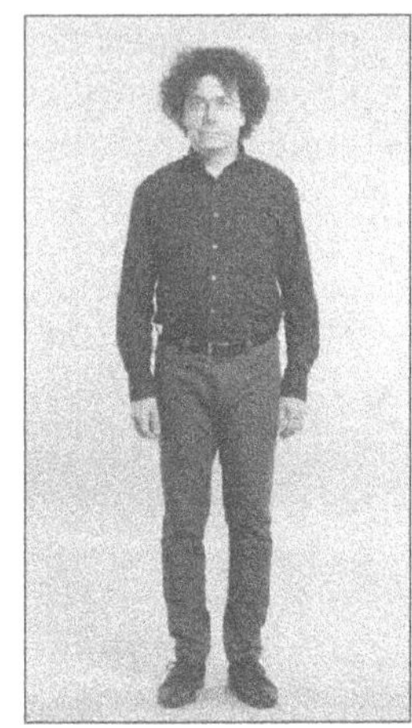

Figure 4c

"I would like my children to live here and feel the house as their own!" (Fig. 4d).

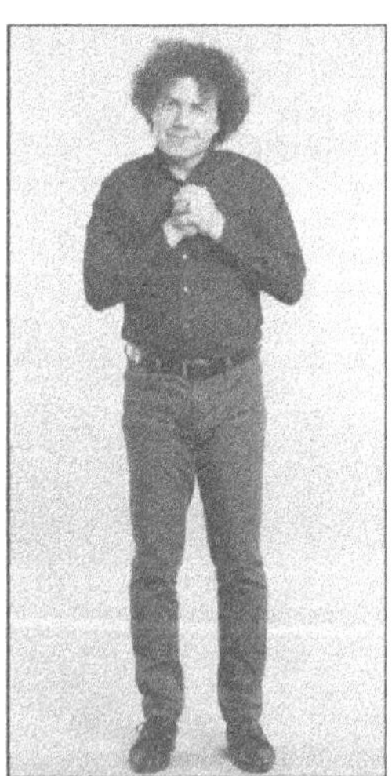
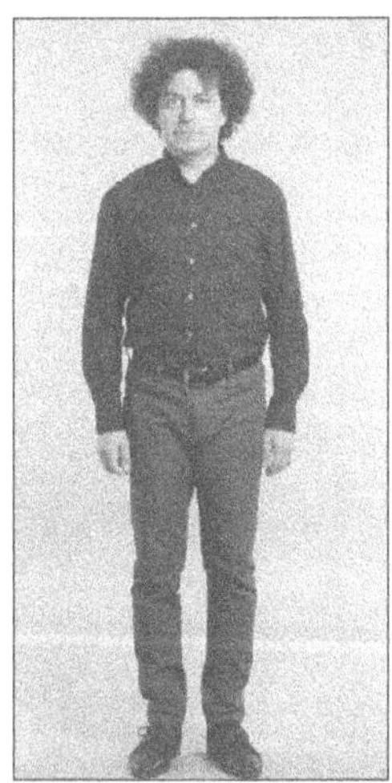

Figure 4d

When we speak we do not separate words by pauses. On the contrary—we merge them together. When we listen to a conversation in a language which we do not know well, there are expressions which we cannot split correctly into words.

The reason for this is the merging of the words. You can try this in the very first conversation you are part of, even in your native language.

"Today while I was travelling on the bus I saw this extra ordinary girl"—this is the way we speak. The last example provided proves that what has been said is not a phrase. Notice that after every gesture the hands drop to their initial position by your hips. In real life this is unrealistic. Nobody talks or gestures by separate words and signs. Everything is merged together. Everything moves from one word to another and from one gesture into another in the smoothest and most natural way. This is the normal behavior when you communicate.

Here is the example without "splitting" the phrase in the gesticulation:

"I live in a house" (Fig. 5a).

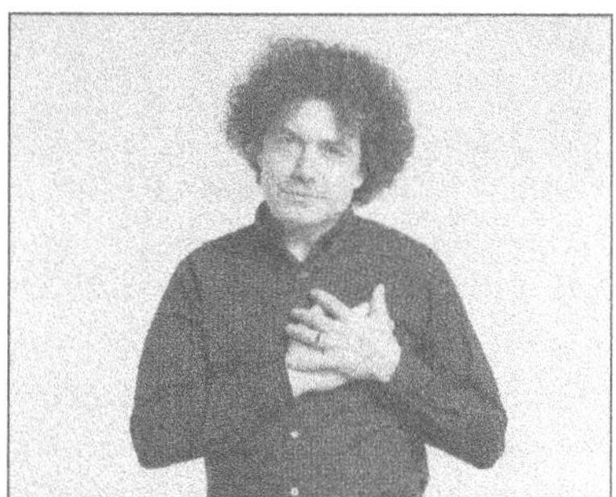

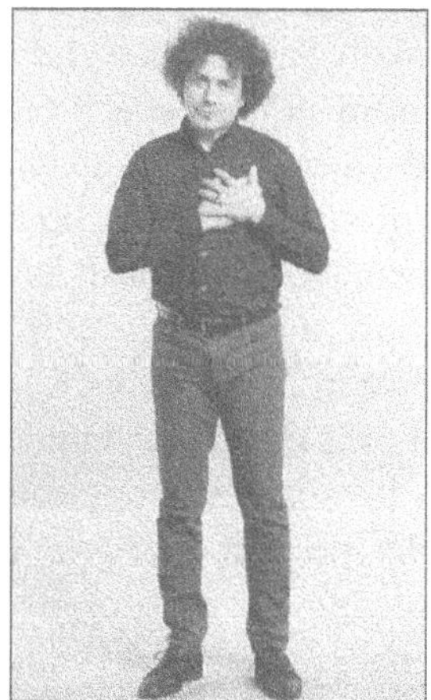

Figure 5a

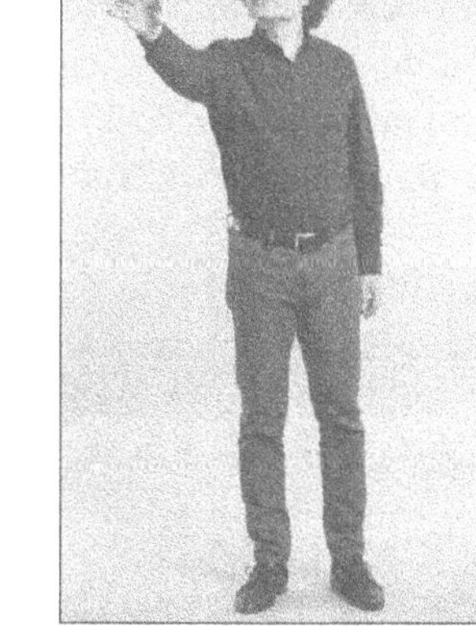

Figure 5b

"The river of my childhood runs by it" (Fig. 5b).

"The river of my first love" (Fig. 5c).

"I would like my children to live here and feel the house as their own!" (Fig. 5d).

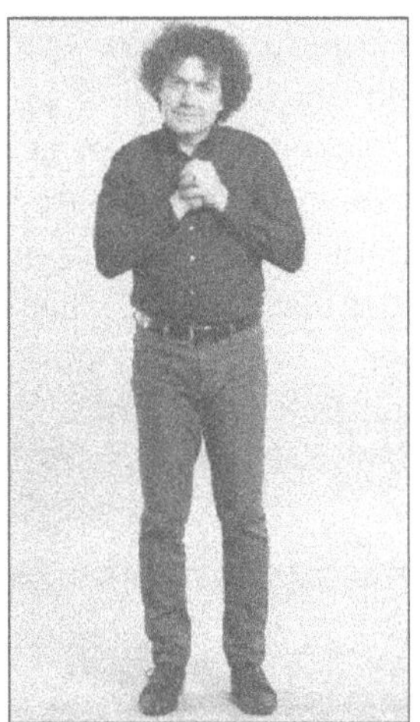
Figure 5c

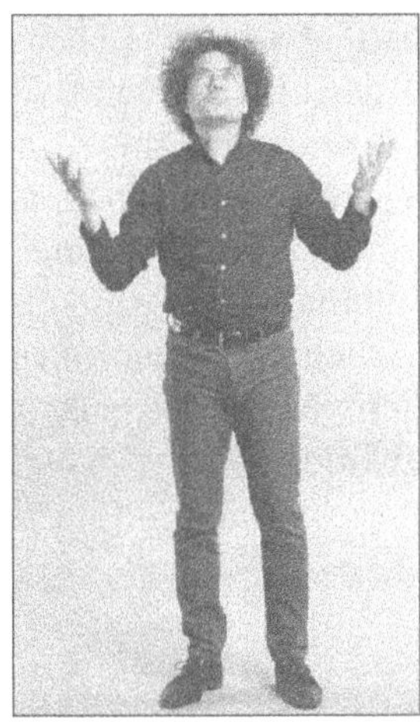
Figure 5d

The example is one of all other possible interpretations of the particular text as far as gestures go.

5.3 Every individual has different physical dimensions. One may be tall, another short, a third strong and a fourth thin, etc. Our gesticulatory tendencies, plus our body differences, define our individual mannerisms. National and family peculiarities are part of it, so is the upbringing. Many factors may influence our performance and distinguish us from others: specific things happening at the very moment like worry, stage dimensions, position on the stage, costumes, makeup, etc. We must by no means try to imitate another individual. We must not repeat gestures which are not ours! If you do not know what to do with your hands—it is better to do *nothing*! Behave in a natural way. Do not dissect the air because you have been told that your hands must do something. Do not make grimaces because someone told you the face must be "alive"! Besides the normal gestures which anyone would make while talking or singing, we need to look into the so-called parasitic gestures. These are gestures which do not belong to the context of our performance. It might be a gesture whose endless repetition has turned into an obstacle or is meaningless. This is a gesture which is illogical and inadequate to our general performance on the stage.

Examples

1. Remember the great Whitney Houston—she used to rhythmically open and close her fingers over the mike. This is a typical case of a parasitical gesture (https://www.youtube.com/watch?v=dQ5rJE-KWJg—active as of 23.02.2015).
2. Mariah Carey uses her free hand to show the direction of the melody of her song. Does that really mean anything? (https://www.youtube.com/watch?v=Cd9rQ5pu3m8—active as of 23.02.2015).
3. Another very frequent gesture is holding our free hand in a horizontal position and keeping it like that.
4. Holding the microphone with both hands is one of those parasitic gestures which is part of a group of gestures—of those which try to hide the fact we do not know what to do with the free hand and with stage fever. (https://www.youtube.com/watch?v=tTuLrZkKF8I—active as of 23.02.2015).
5. Holding the cord with your free hand is similar to the gesture described above.
6. Holding the hands all the time at the side of the body or clamped in front of it—this is common for opera singers. It is a gesture which may be called a parasitic one, as it does not contribute to the performer's "story" and hinders body movement. The performer is also paralyzed, as the brain receives a signal of purposeful passive behavior of the hands. (https://www.youtube.com/watch?v=JlSodSvo1Lg—active as of 23.02.2015).

See more at: www.martinkarnolsky.com

The examples of parasitic gestures are endless. There are also UGLY gestures. For example, pointing your finger at someone. It is all the more ugly if we are telling someone we love them. It is highly doubtful that this is the most beautiful gesture to express our love. What we are talking about here is necessary tactfulness, of taking the time to think it over. Sufficient preparation provides us with enough gestures to use during our performance. Communication with the audience is the same as when we are with friends or strangers or all kinds of interlocutors. The big difference stems from the need to be more brilliant in expression. Often hyperbolic in behavior. This is because the big stage "engulfs" us and the people in the back rows will not notice a nod or a slight movement of the fingers. The problem is solved by big screens which show us in close ups. This is not the case at every concert, however.

Besides parasitic and ugly gestures, there are inadequate gestures. The meanings of a number of gestures differ with various cultures and people. For example, the thumbs up sign means *ok* for a lot of people, but Greeks understand it as "Shut up!" The head movement for "yes" and "no" is different for Bulgarians in comparison to other people. Many humorous situations occur because of people having misunderstood our yes for a no. We just need to bear in mind these peculiarities when we face an international audience.

How should we select our behavior and gestures, in particular, for a specific performance? Before answering this, we need some clarifications:

What is the nature of the hall or podium?

Who are the audience?

What is on stage—technical equipment, instruments, etc.?

Is there enough time and possibility for costume change?

Are we alone on stage or with an accompanying group, a ballet, etc.?

Is it a day or an evening performance?

What is the reason for the spectacle—a political, charity, or individual (commercial) show, etc.?

The answers to these and other questions provide us the idea of the concert in which we will participate or perform alone. They allow us to select the behavior for each song. To select the costume, lights, dancers and what not. You all know these aspects but we need to repeat and systematize them. On the other hand, I want to lead you in a natural way to what I have to say about the fact that each actor needs to have at least 2 or 3 variants of his performance. What if you have sing on a small club stage and you have rehearsed on a big one? Wouldn't your performance be somewhat lame or inadequate? What if you rehearsed with a band which plays live music only and suddenly you have to appear on the stage alone? This may happen for a number of reasons—because of TV, because of no sound equipment for the band. Wouldn't that also be inadequate? Here is the conclusion we arrive at:

When we have gathered the full information on the conditions in which the concert will be held we begin taking them into consideration and reformatting the performance. This is the general approach. I would go even further—we need a synonymous gesture for everything. If we are on a small stage and we have no possibility of running or dancing, we need to work on the same character at the rehearsals but presented with different gestures. We need to perform in a way which will allow the song and the behavior to be recognized by previous viewers and they will see our natural performance in different circumstances.

We have special cases when a part of the lyrics is repeated in the song multiple times. In this situation we should be ready with a number of synonymous gestures in order not to look like parrots. The gestures may be only a few but repeated in an order which the audience will not recognize. Some of them may be omitted or we can use some small tricks, so that our presentation will be interesting as stage behavior.

5.4 There are some Behavior Peculiarities Which We Know and Which We can Profit by. In our genetic memory we have engraved gestures and behavior models from the time when it was more important and decisive for communication between us. For example, if we are afraid or stressed the brain immediately sends a signal to the body to protect ourselves. One of the most natural gestures of the hands is to move them in front of the torso at breast level. This is a position for defense or attack.

If we want only to protect ourselves, our hands will automatically move to the neck and the face. Or to the chest. Those who wish to show that they are not afraid do exactly the opposite. They take an open position and show the soft body parts—the neck, the belly and the genitals. To stress this even more I will point to how grown men start a conflict which threatens to develop into a fight. They lift their chest up, all the body muscles are tense. Often, at a very close distance or, as we say, in the intimate space of the opponent, they will start hitting their chests—this is opposite to showing fear. But we are on the stage—is it appropriate to behave like roosters? Most probably not. We will show no aggression. In most cases we will show the body parts mentioned and will open our palms (Fig. 6). The latter with the purpose of manifesting "we are unarmed," we do not pose a threat to anybody. We trust the audience will understand the muted response (see Allan Pease and Alan Garner, *Body Language. Talk Language*).

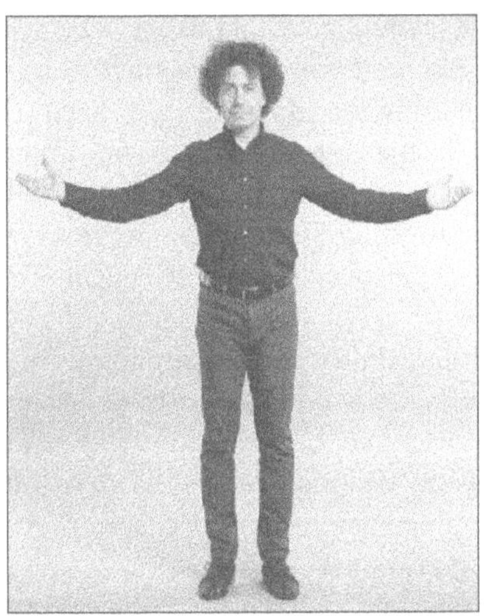

Figure 6

The elbows must not be in front of the torso—this is another useful position of the hands (Fig. 7). The elbows must not be stuck to it on the sides (Fig. 8). There should be a distance of two or three fingers between the elbows and the torso (Fig. 9).

Taking our position on the stage. we also need to think about body weight. It is not our personal weight we have in mind. The stage has seen overweight and thin singers and actors, but this is not what is most important. Depending on the song, we need to consider which leg carries the bigger weight. For example, if we protect ourselves, the weight will go to the back leg (Fig. 10).

If we need to manifest zeal and readiness, the weight will be on the front leg (Fig. 11). If we want to show stability, the legs should be on one line and the weight will be split equally between the two (Fig. 12).

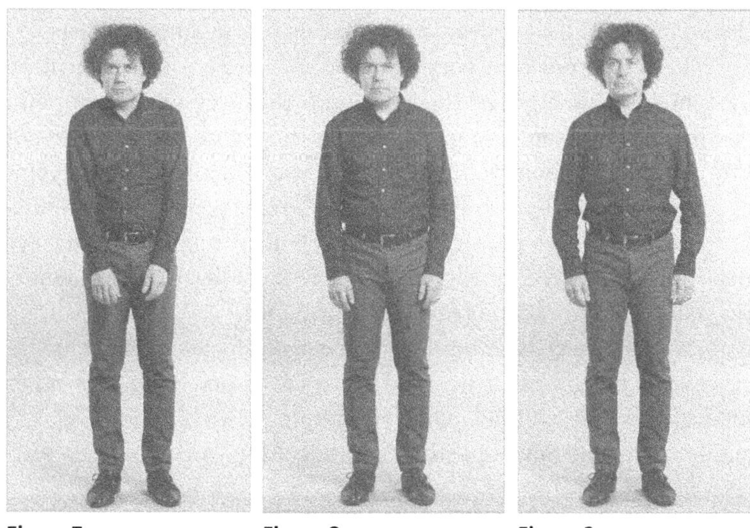

Figure 7 **Figure 8** **Figure 9**

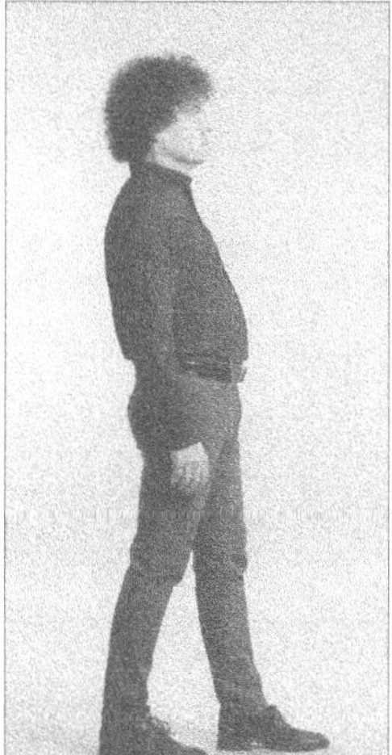

Figure 10

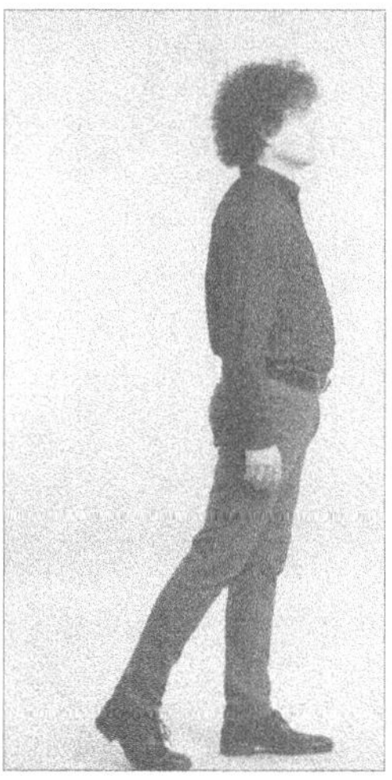

Figure 11

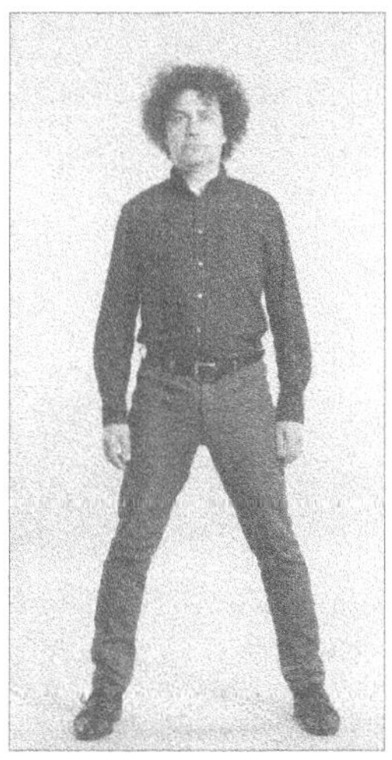

Figure 12

We have been emphasizing so far on the position of the torso straight in the direction of the central part of the audience. Please pay attention to the position of the palms. They are as important as the face, the legs and all other parts of the body. It is no secret that hand gestures are innumerable. And it is a fact that the hands are the most developed instruments in human beings.

The hands perform very delicate as also very rude activities. The most frequently used gestures are those by which we point to someone or something. Pointing a finger at someone is not the prettiest or most polite gesture to use. Then how do we point at someone and tell them we love them? I refer you to the beginning of the chapter—the gesture shall complement the word! What we need to do is add a quality to make it more beautiful, widening the palette of impressions in our performance.

How can we confess our love and use our hands to assist us?

Let us imagine that we hold the mike in one hand. The other hand is free. We will not point at anything with a finger (Fig. 13) similar to the old Soviet poster "Comrade, have you voted?"

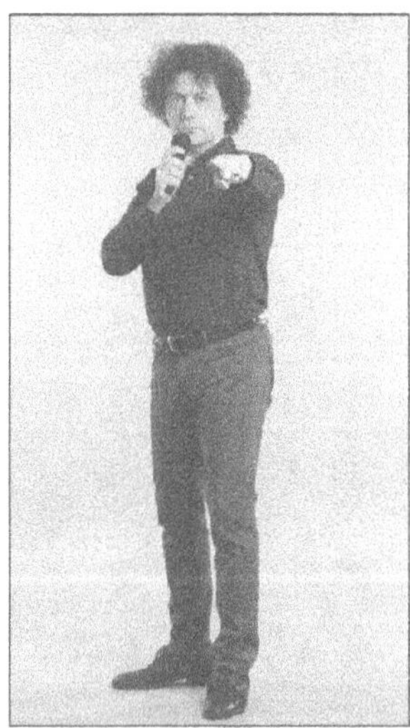

Figure 13

No! When feelings are at play we must be very careful and pay attention to every detail.

Here is an example: Figs. 14a–c.

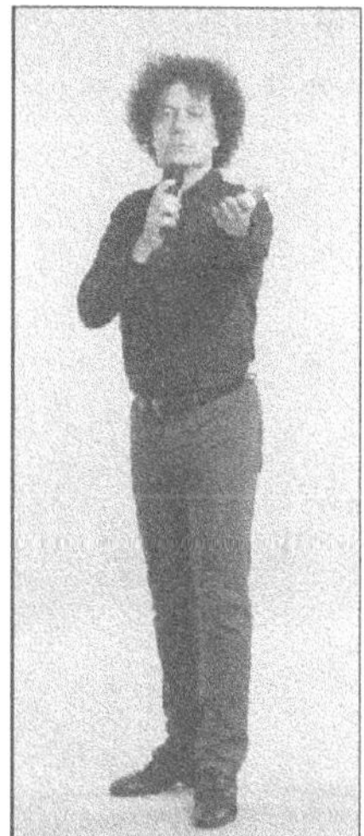

Figure 14a

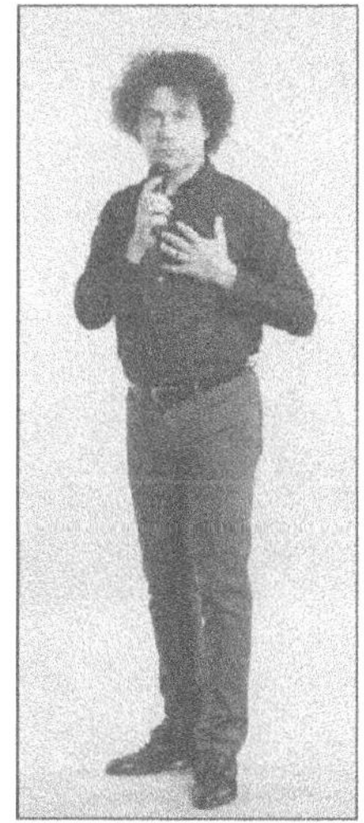

Figure 14b

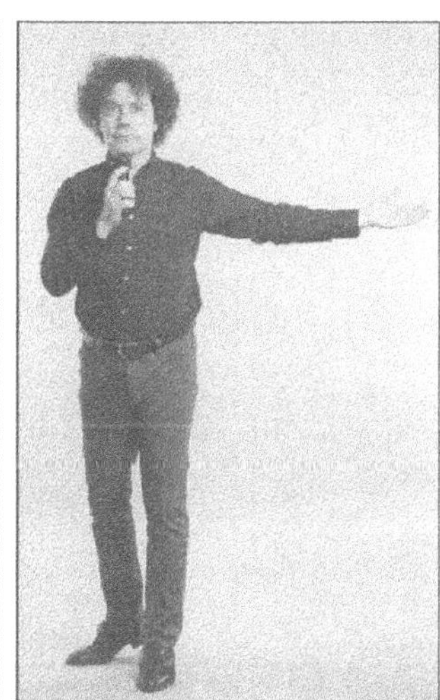

Figure 14c

We can see that the position of the hand is palm up (Fig. 14a). It means that we give something additional to the declaration of love. Be it our heart or our trust. The variants depend on the general idea of the text. This gesture may be finished by a movement to our heart (Fig. 14b). Or by opening the hand horizontally, so that we are fully open (Fig. 14c). I repeat, it depends on the text and how we interpret it.

We can also tell someone about our love, but the palm may be pointing downwards (Fig. 15a).

This is more a "stop" signal. The reason is that the slightest movement of the fingers upwards will turn it into an explicit attempt to stop someone moving in our direction. If the text is about our beloved at a moment of separation and if it includes a declaration of love, then the gesture might be fine. To complete the phrase of the gesture, we can turn the head to one side (Fig. 15b).

In this way we refuse the visual contact with the "object" we talk to. In this case—with the audience. What if we move the hand in a direction opposite to the direction of the look? Will our refusal be not very categorical, if followed by a declaration of love? (Fig. 15c)?

What we have to remember is that only by moving the palm upwards or downwards will the quality of the expression "I love you" change. If we move forward with the palm pointing down (Fig. 15d) we do not stop anybody—we try to reach the object of the declaration.

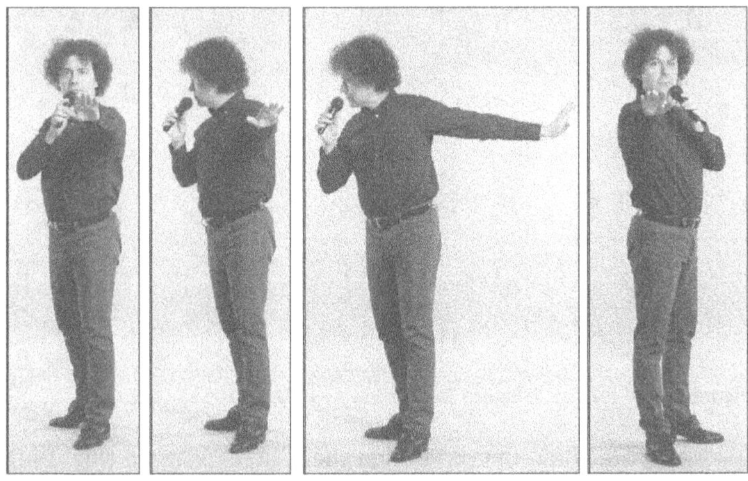

Figure 15a **Figure 15b** **Figure 15c** **Figure 15d**

This is the third way of development in the situation. Whatever we do, it must be logical and transfer smoothly from one gesture to another, from one phrase to another.

Conclusion

The gesture is a means of non-verbal communication among people in which, by way of symbolic movements, an idea or meaning is expressed. The movement is done most often with the hands and the head, but also with the body. This type of movement is called gesticulation. The gesture must complement the word and not repeat it! With a gesture we may change the meaning of the words.

The gesture must enhance and elaborate the information of a selected "strong" word and add more features to the word. It may come before, with or after the word. The other variants are mixed and follow out of the three mentioned so far. There may be a gesture which will start before a specific word, will last while we pronounce it and stay on after it. Or start before it and finish simultaneously or start together with the word and finish after it.

A "phrase in the gesture" is a sequence in the gesture, complete in its meaning.

A parasitic gesture is one which does not belong to the context of our performance. It might be a gesture whose endless repetition has turned into an obstacle or is meaningless. This is a gesture which is illogical and inadequate to our general presentation on the stage.

With "inadequate gestures" the meanings differ with various cultures and people.

"Ugly" gestures do not correspond to the generally accepted moral and esthetic norms in society. For example: pointing a finger at someone or gestures which may be offensive on religious or sexual grounds.

We define the gestures to be used for a specific performance. They depend on a number of factors:

What is the hall or podium where we perform?

Who are the audience?

What will there be on stage—technical equipment, instruments, etc.?

Is there enough time and possibility for costume change?

Are we alone on stage or with an accompanying group, a ballet troupe, etc.?

Is it a day or evening performance?

What is the reason for the spectacle—a political, charity, individual (commercial) show, etc.?

"Synonymous gestures" are different in performance and can be added to a strong word without changing the general meaning and purpose of the presentation. They are used to introduce variety in cases of repeated gestures or for convenience and expedience to match different stages, surroundings, etc.

Depending on the song context, we select: the position of the body, the center of weight, position of the hands, direction of the palms and other aspects, all aimed at creating the character as desired by the performer and suggesting a certain message to the audience.

Chapter 6

The Look

In this chapter you will learn about the *look* and about some techniques of contact with the audience. You will understand what the "*phrase in the look*" is all about. We will also deal with behavior in front of the camera while on stage.

The look of the actor is an instrument to establish direct contact with the audience. For the performer the most fearful aspect is to look the audience in the eye. But if we learn how to do it in a convincing way and use it so that the audience shifts its look away from us, then there is no audience in the world which will not believe our message from the stage. Actually, examples abound in every frame of any concert. Pay attention to the singers who hide behind closed eyes. In most cases they also hold the microphone with both hands.

Let us elaborate on that: what is the meaning of singing with your eyes closed? If we refer once again to body language we will see that this is one of the first and most inborn gestures of man—hiding. To prove it, let us see how a child will hide if we are in the same room. It is simple. The principle is if he does not see us, we do not see him.

Stage Performance for Singers: A Practical Course in 12 Basic Steps
Martin Karnolsky

ISBN 978-981-4800-20-4 (Paperback), 978-0-429-42869-2 (eBook)
www.panstanford.com

He closes his eyes and that is it. The child may even press his palms on the eyes. Just to make sure he has hidden well.

Let us take another example. Do you remember how many times you have told someone or heard the phrase "Look into my eyes when I am talking to you!"? Why? Do you not know or hear the source of information? Or when you have been reprimanded, when you have worried about a mistake or a poor evaluation?

I strongly believe that everything said so far is clear. Do not forget to use this instrument—the look—to establish direct contact with the audience and to be persuasive.

Here are some wrong directions in that look; of course this is relative and depends on the character. There is no character in suggesting lack of respect of the audience in the hall!

We see a gaze at the floor of the stage (Fig. 1). It is doubtful whether this is preferable to closed eyes, but it is quite common. In particular, with beginners. They select a spot on the floor of the hall or of the stage and this is all they do with their look. I feel the person "*must* finish this singing job" in front of an audience. And a part of these singers will literally undergo a transformation when the song ends. They smile, look in a normal way to the audience. Others . . . well, they just run away from the stage.

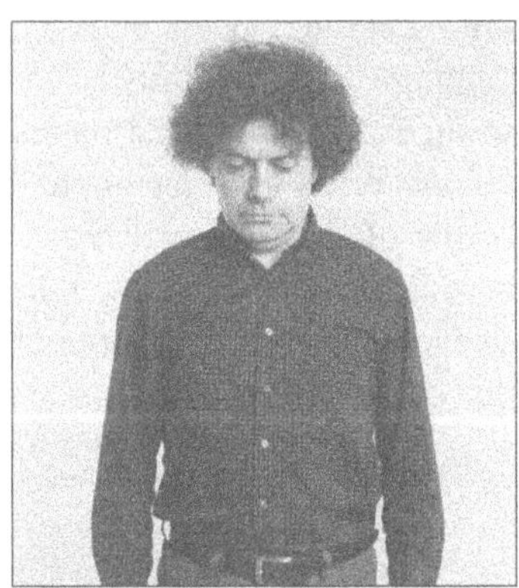

Figure 1

In Fig. 2 the look is radial. The ceiling or the sky on the open stage are as inacceptable variants of looks as the stage floor.

You will never be credible to the audience, if while sharing something from your heart, you look at the ceiling. On the contrary—the listener will be bored; he will be distracted. The basic feeling is that of lack of respect. The audience will be left with the impression that you fear and disrespect them. What will you then get in return? The same reaction—that lack of respect.

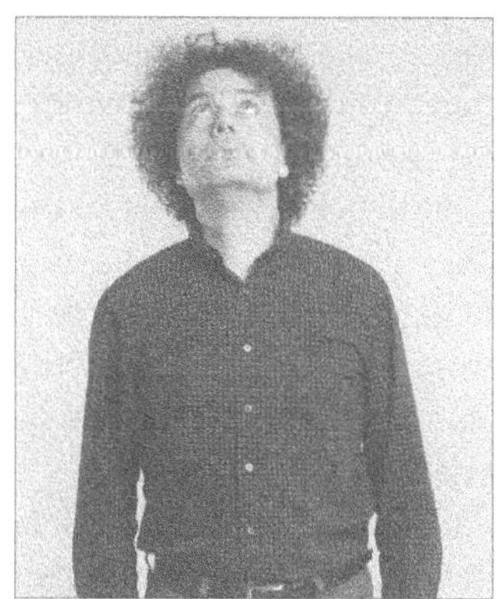
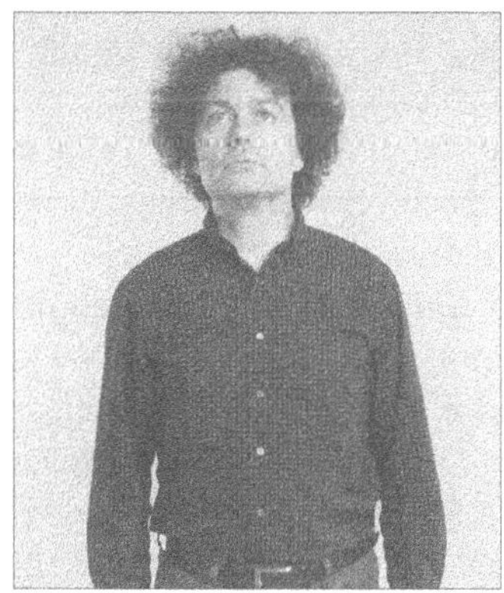

Figure 2

The case of Fig. 3 is identical with the above. It does not matter whether you look upwards or sideways. The feeling of the audience will be the same—disrespect, fear, and unaware of what to do with their eyes—irrespective of whether you look at the floor, the sky, the ceiling, the right or left part of the hall.

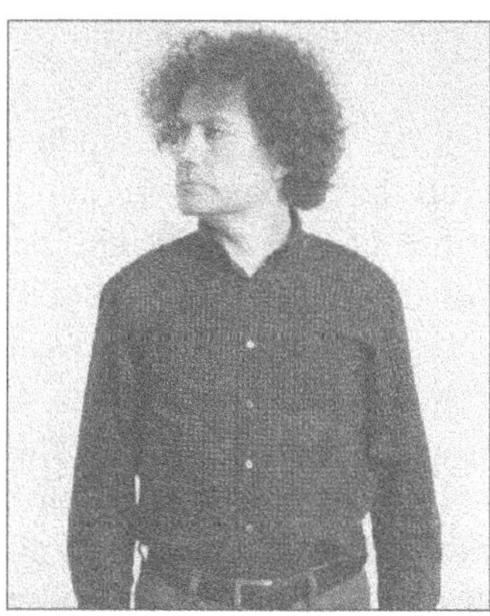
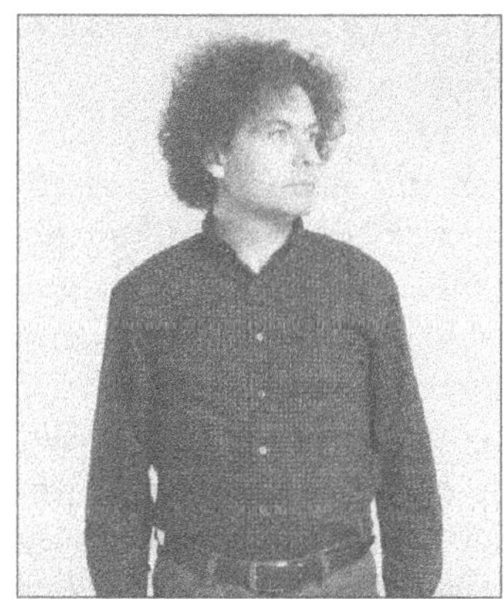

Figure 3

The major task of the look is to establish contact with the audience. The first and basic contact happens via the look. With our very first steps on stage or with the first tones sung, we contact the audience via the *look*. We have already discussed the situation when the actor performs a song or a text with closed eyes. Hidden behind himself and in himself, he is calm, believing "nobody sees him." This is wrong! They are mere excuses to be living the part and the song, pretenses to make the performance more emotional! If I want to *only* listen to music, I will switch on the radio. At a concert I expect to see a show. To see that the actor respects me and looks at me (the audience). I expect normal communication! I have mentioned normal communication several times. We are people who walk out on the stage to tell a story. This means that we are meeting someone to talk with, to share thoughts and feelings. We must do nothing which would not look natural. We need to converse naturally.

So far we have discussed the need of contact with the audience. How do we do that? It is simple. Step one: if the conditions on the stage are perfect we should not see the audience. Yes. We will not see them if the lights have been correctly installed, sufficiently powerful and of good quality from the artistic point of view. If everything is perfect, there will be a light wall in front of us, separating us from the audience. What is this light wall? It is the effect of the lights which have "flooded" the stage to a degree which does not allow us to see anything happening in the hall. This may raise questions, however.

Is this not the moment when we have the effect of the "closed eyes"?

Yes, but we still have to consider the fact that the audience sees the singer and *perfectly well* at that! So, this is not the effect of "closed eyes," as the performer does not look like he is hidden. On the contrary, now the question is how to establish eye contact with the audience. This contact will be missing, practically, as there is no feedback about the audience reaction to the performance. The absence of information does not mean the performer is excused from the obligation to present himself most convincingly and convey his ideas to the audience. We need a categorical answer to the question how the singer will manage his "blindness" in such a manner as not to allow anybody to understand that he does not see the audience. Let us remember what we said about the look and the gestures.

The singer will have to perform everything that has been prepared during the rehearsals, thinking of the spots left and right on the stage, of the central part, etc.—this has been discussed above.

One more question: how can we gauge if the audience likes us and reacts positively to what we do? I doubt that there is a correct answer to this question, universal as it is. Needless to say, it is all related to the good training of the performer and for the show. It also depends on the experience and on the knowledge of how the audience reacts to our performance.

Next question: what can we do to make people believe we can see them? Here the subject of the look opens in depth.

If you remember in Chapter 2 we spoke about the split of the stage space and of the audience—the latter is split in central, right and left parts. I would like to share several small secrets to help you solve the issue of looking into the eyes of the audience. To begin with: *yes*, we look the audience in the eye. What if we cannot do that? Here is trick No. 1: we look at their foreheads. From the side it seems like we are looking into their eyes. If one person understands that we are not looking into his eyes, all the others will believe we are looking into his eyes. This is exactly what we need—the audience to feel we are looking in their eyes. If you cannot do this, then you can do it in a different way and it will still seem that you are looking into their eyes. Look at eye level, but between the heads of people. Here is an example: if you look between the heads of the people in the 6th row, most probably, because of the usual amphitheatrical arrangement of the seats in the hall and the difference in the height between you and the audience, your look will fall somewhat lower than the faces of the people in the 7th row. To all those looking at you from the side, you will seem to be looking in the eyes of the audience in the 6th row. This is what we needed—and we have got it!

The above technique may also be a special case—you may look into an empty chair between the faces of the people in the front row. However, I do not wish for you empty chairs at your concert!

There is also the technique of the "well-meaning spectator." You may find a relative, a friend or a fan in the audience. Someone who has liked you even before your performance and will send back some positive energy. Someone who supports you and will not betray you if you turn to them. This will give you some time to pull yourself together and gain momentum. Having managed the initial stress and tension, you can start "working" with other people in the audience. These will be people you do not know, but you believe will support you.

It is time to go back to the light curtain. We keep the positions described above in our mind and go back to the rehearsal hall where we have literally trained and memorized the looks to the central part of the audience, then to the left and the right side. This must reach the level at which, when stepping out on a well-lit stage which does not allow you to see the audience, you still behave in a way as if you see the people. The majority of the audience, probably above 95%, do not know that the actors see nothing. It is by no means by chance that at some concerts, predominantly at rock concerts, there are enormous white lights directed at the audience during applause or at selected moments. At this time the singers see the spectators clearly. The rest of the time the actor will find a space between the spotlights and see some silhouettes and even faces, but this happens rarely for the center of the stage and is more true to some of the last seats in the rows. This is why our training must be so good that it enables us to perform in a manner that makes everybody think we see them!

There is one more category of audience which may be in the hall—the TV audience. Or the audience that may see our photos. When the TV cameras are situated in the hall, their small red lights are on during transmission to the mobile TV station where the video and sound signals are mixed. If there are only video cameras they also have small red lamps which are on during the recording.

It is not easy to take into consideration all these million things which may happen on stage, but there is no excuse. We have to try and pay attention to these cameras. They are the "eyes" of the TV audience. Through them we can convey our message to people who are not present in the hall. A message which stays much longer than the one to the immediate audience in the hall as a video recording can be watched many times over, while the live performance cannot be repeated. Thus everything said about working with the look with the audience in the hall is fully in force and also applies to the work with the camera.

Last but not least, let us define what "the phrase in the look" is. A phrase in the look is a sequence of looks which have a complete meaning. Here is an example:

"Well, let us go to the shop and buy (Fig. 4a)

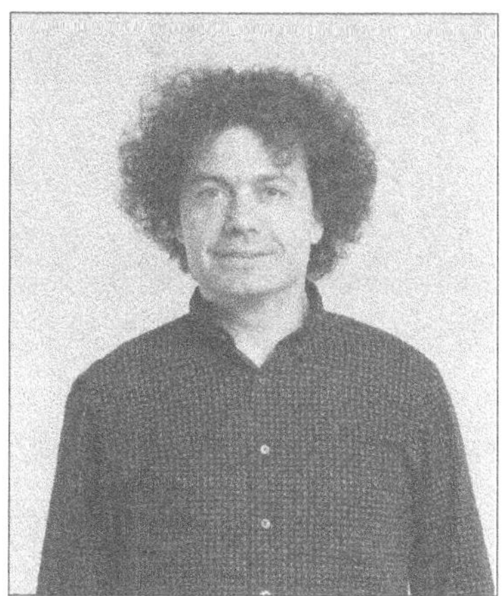

Figure 4a

... three packs of milk, some salami and some bread (Fig. 4b)

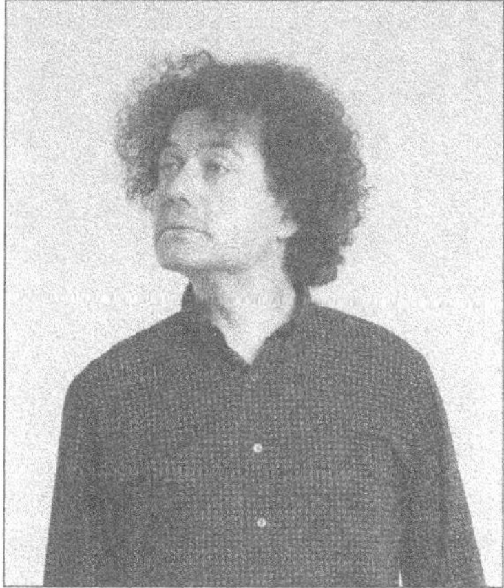

Figure 4b

... after that we can go to my place and (Fig. 4c)

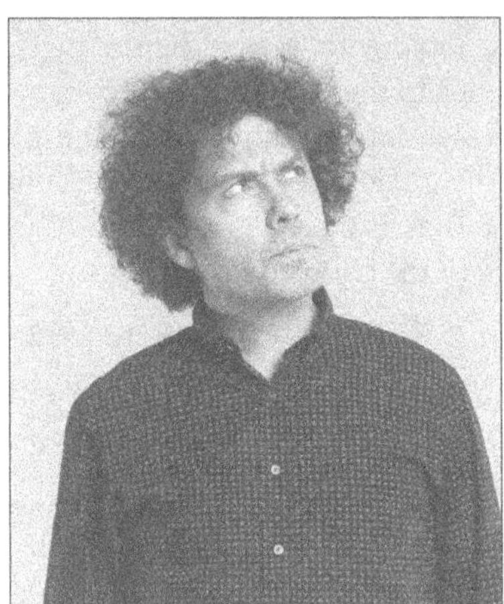

Figure 4c

... make some sandwiches (Fig. 4d)."

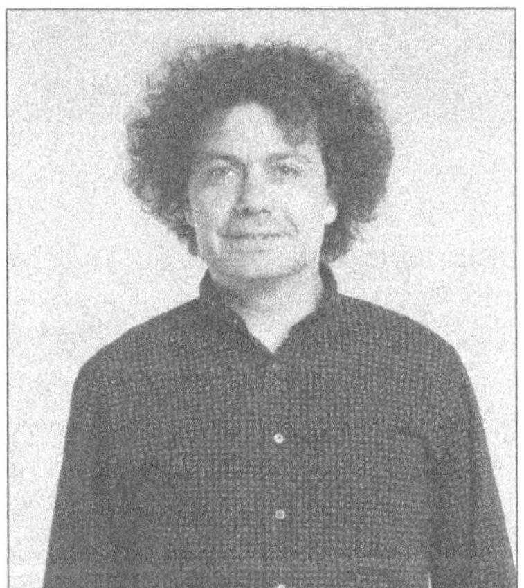

Figure 4d

What can we see here? At the outset the look is directed at the interlocutor. When we list the products to be bought from the shop the eyes move, the hands count the number of products while we think over what to buy and how much of it to buy. Then we return to the interlocutor and we finish the phrase—in the text, in the gesture and most important—in the look—when we suggest what to prepare from these products.

When we start a sentence looking at someone in the audience we must close it when looking at the same person. The whole phrase must be logical! We cannot address John when looking at George, Michael, Ben and John one after the other. Even if we forget what we talked about with each of them and when, when we look in front of us and start a new phrase we close it as we look at the same person or point of the "light curtain." Only then everything will seem natural and logical! Only then will we have the feeling of natural communication with the audience. Imagine that when you face the audience it will be composed of no more than 4 or 5 people. You will have to turn to the left and to the right. Do not do anything different from a normal talk in a group! This conversation will give you the opportunity to overcome the fear of where to, how and how long to look in order to appear at your best!

When you master the techniques of communication with the look, your stage presence will be drastically improved! The audience will like you more. Do not spare any effort! Stand in front of the mirror and try gestures, looks, poses. Rehearse them! This job is very simple. Even boring, not very pleasant, but really necessary!

How do magicians perform their tricks? We all know that they lie to us. We all know that the rabbit is hidden somewhere. Why do we not see how the magician takes it out of a secret pocket? It is very simple—they look at what they want us to look at. They make some distracting movements, tell us stories and so on, but all the time they gaze at a point which is far from the secret pocket where the rabbit is hidden. And what do we do? We look where they look. If you do not believe me, then during a conversation try this technique: while you are talking to a person or while they are talking to you, look at some distant spot from time to time. To make the effect stronger, you can half close your eyes as if you are focusing or staring at the "thing." I assure you that at the third or fourth look the other person will turn to see what you are looking at. So we can conclude that my words are right—people look where you look!

Conclusion

What is the look and what is its role in our artistic performance? It is the instrument which establishes direct contact with the audience, which suggests to the audience that we are on the stage because we know what we do there and what we want to say.

Working with the camera is as important as working with the audience. The principles are the same. The problem is the absence of feedback from the audience, but this should not influence our performance, as it has been prepared beforehand and is perfect.

The phrase in the look is a sequence of looks which have a complete meaning and flow logically from one another and closes itself in the gesture and the text.

Chapter 7

The Phrase in the Gesture and the Look

In this chapter we will discuss the phrase in the gesture and in the look. We will also define what the most appropriate level of gesticulation is.

What is the phrase in the gesture and the look? This is a sequence of gestures and looks which follow logically one after the other and represent a complete thought.

Let us interpret it. I remind you that there is a missing component—the text. When we talk about the text we will return to the phrase in the gesture and the look.

Do you remember the chapter on gestures and the example of the house?

"I live in a house (Fig. 1a).

(We start the phrase directed at someone, looking into their eyes.)

. . . Sometimes I have to go to the shop which is quite far away (Fig. 1b) . . .

(As we can see the hand keeps pointing at the house while the look is in the direction of the shop.)

Stage Performance for Singers: A Practical Course in 12 Basic Steps
Martin Karnolsky

ISBN 978-981-4800-20-4 (Paperback), 978-0-429-42869-2 (eBook)
www.panstanford.com

. . . I walk home carrying all the purchases (Fig. 1c)."

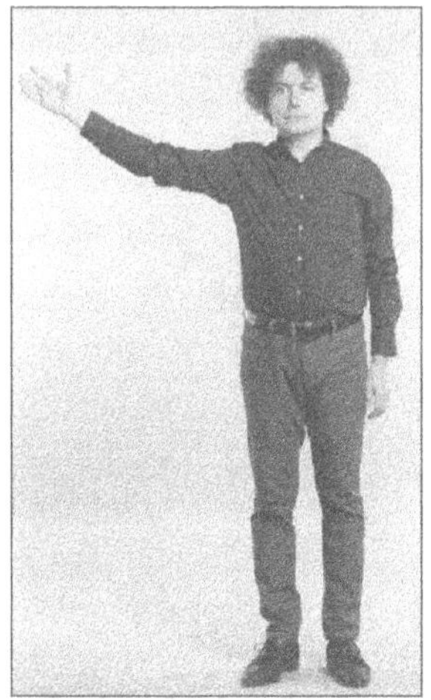

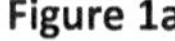

Figure 1a

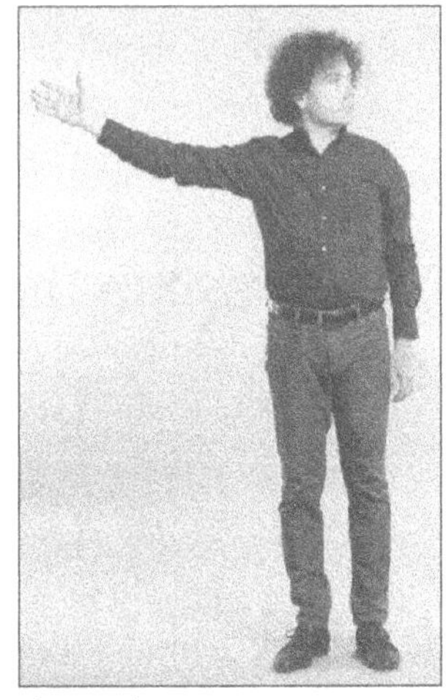

Figure 1b

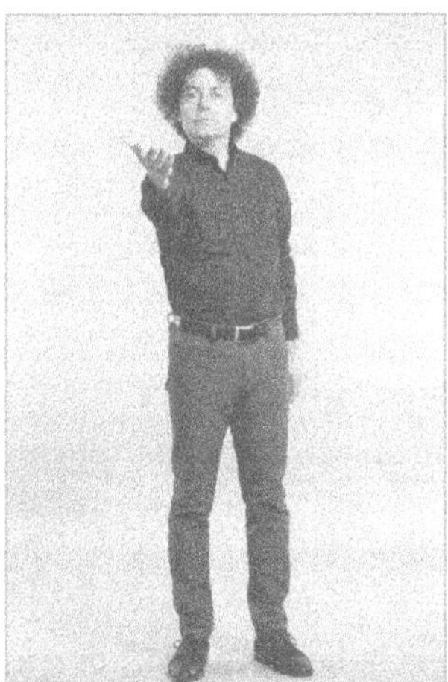

Figure 1c

(We finish the phrase in the direction of the person we are talking to by turning back the look and, as you can see in the photo, the gesture is also at them.)

We must not forget that the look and the gesture are unbreakably linked together. They "live" together, "breathe" together and are actually one entity. No way would they be different. If we can say something with a gesture, we have to refer it to someone or something and turn to the interlocutor. You express an attitude even if you do not look someone in the eye. Having dedicated separate chapters to both the gesture and the look, we need not dwell on that any further.

What we need to define here is the height of the gestures we make. As the eyes that watch us must stay under control, we have no right to lose contact with the audience for long and unreasonable periods of time. If we turn our look away, it must be for a short time only, so as not to allow the audience to be bored by the fact that we do not look at them. People should not think that we mean any disrespect. The sense of proportion comes with family upbringing, stage experience, life experience, etc. and reflects on our behavior in many ways. It can be learnt too.

What is the height at which we gesture? If we are looking at the eyes of a person and are standing upright, all gestures below the waist and even somewhat higher will not be visible to viewers except if their look turns away from our eyes. They will look down. But we do not want the interlocutor to lose focus! We must keep the eyes of our audience focused on our face as much as we can. What if we raise our hands too high? At the least, it will look funny. The hands will somehow be waving to somebody.

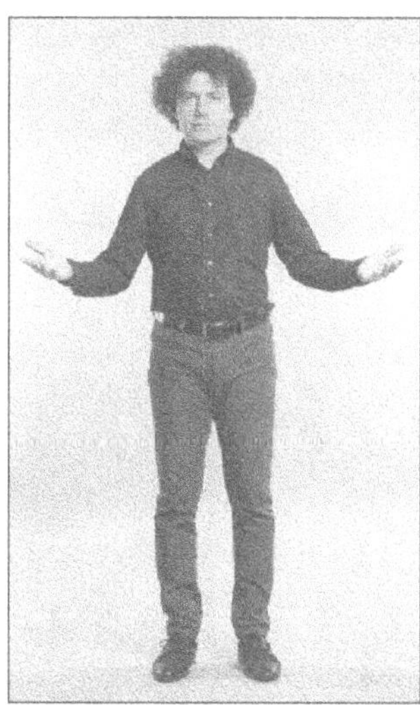

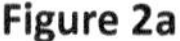

Figure 2a

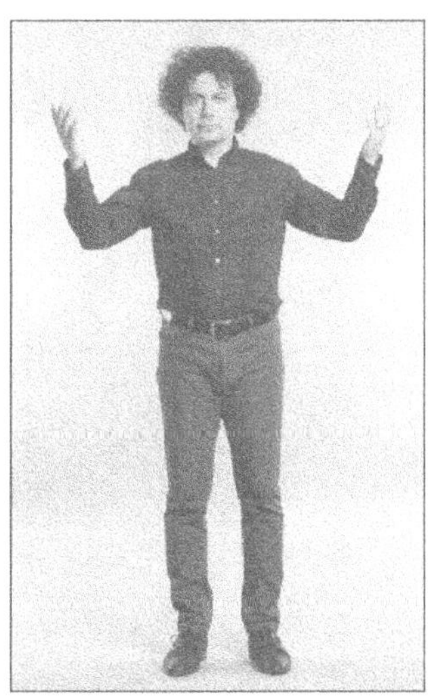

Figure 2b

Our hand gestures must be minimum at the height of the elbows and not higher than the chin. Why is that? Because at this level we enter the peripheral vision zone of the performer and the spectators with distracting movements. If we lift our hands above the chin, we may hide our faces. Thus this is the range which we may use horizontally (Figs. 2a and b).

This allows us to split the types of gestures by height—low, middle, high and super high (Figs. 3a–d). By volume and dynamics, gestures can be split into small, middle and big, or gestures of low, middle and high dynamics.

Do not misunderstand the above and think that the hands should never be raised above the chin or higher. No! We are talking here about the basic number of gestures. If you need to put an accent or, in the moment of culmination, to raise your hand vertically and to a maximum height—you are welcome! However, the gestures above the said level must not be too many. The effect will be lost. And how much more would we be able to raise our hand at the culmination? There may be exceptions related to some sort of choreography or a movement above the level of the chin. Or even above the head (Figs. 4a–c).

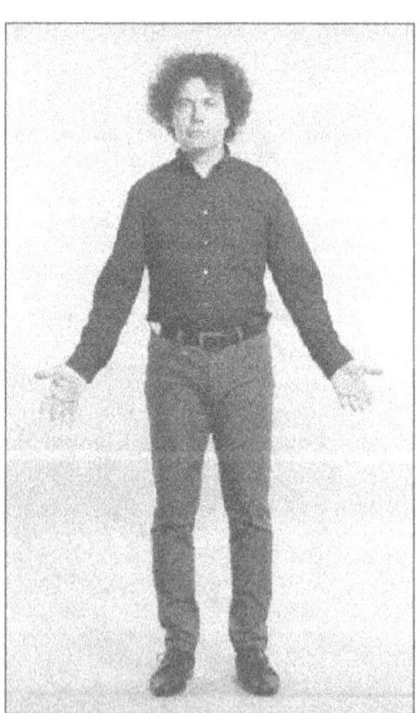

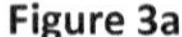

Figure 3a

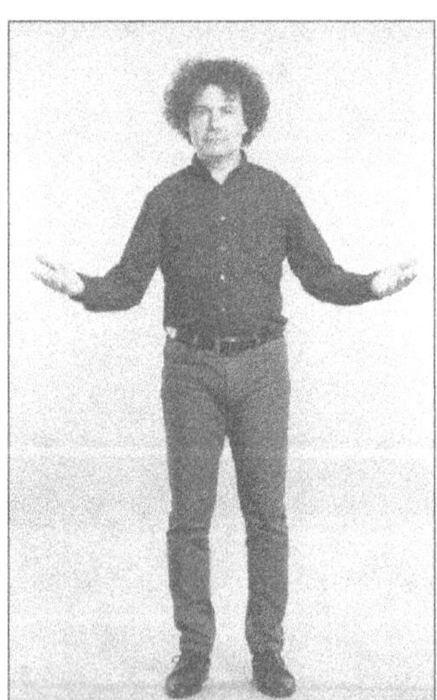

Figure 3b

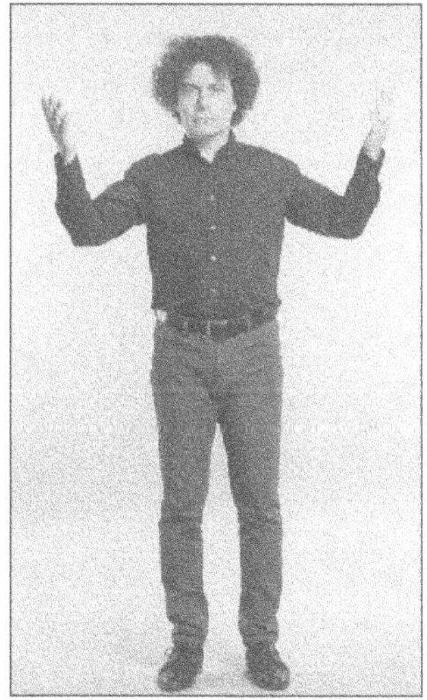
Figure 3c

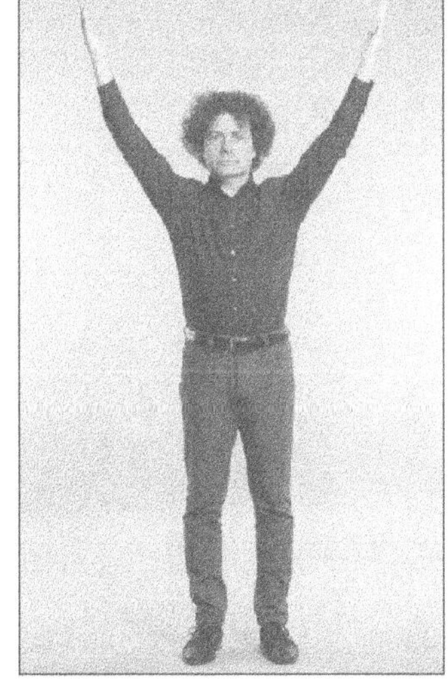
Figure 3d

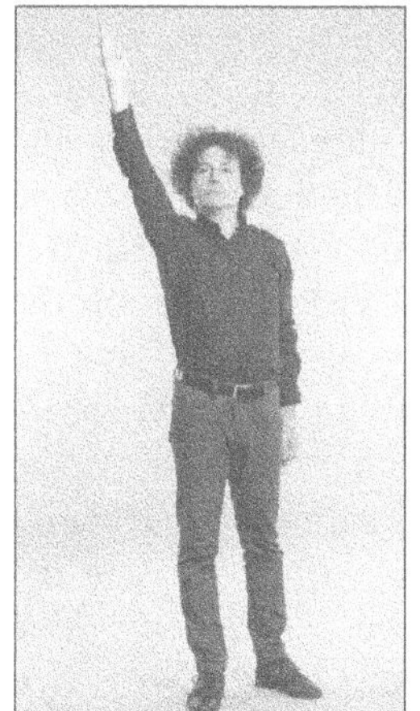
Figure 4a

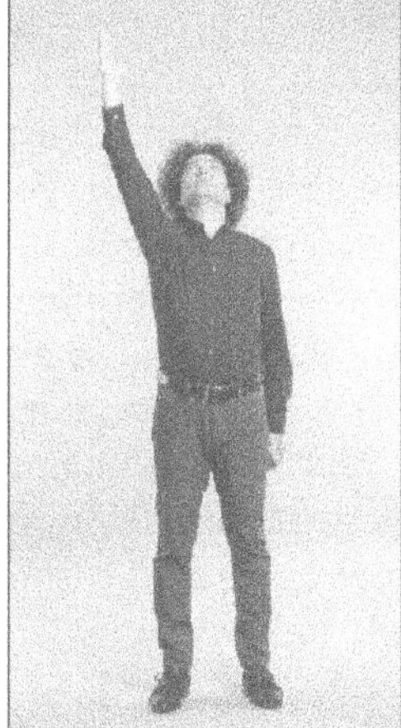
Figure 4b

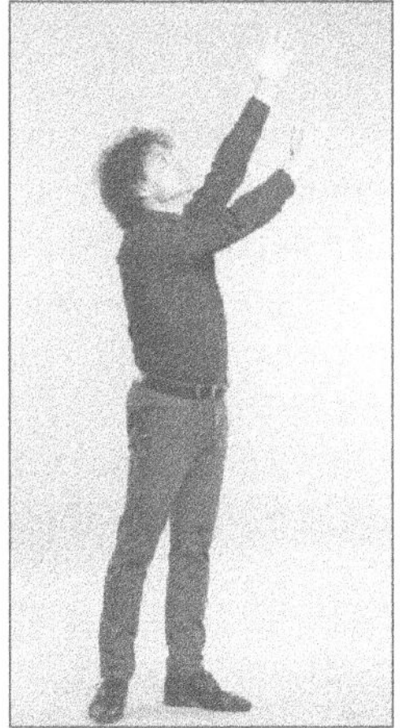
Figure 4c

The same is true about gestures below elbow level. First, they are lower than the peripheral vision zone and second, they are smaller and invisible.

To a great degree they look passive and incidental (Figs. 5a–c).

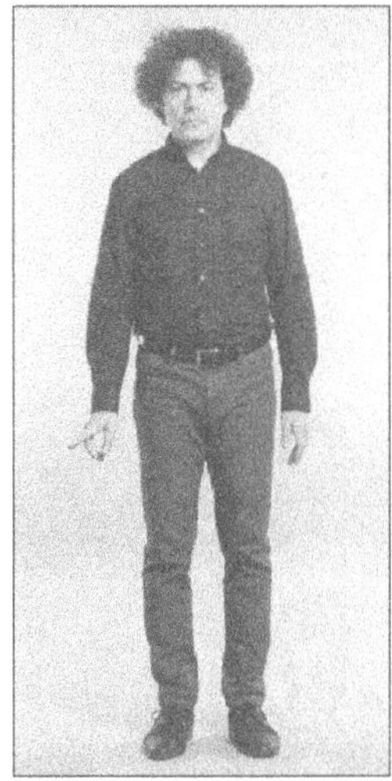
Figure 5a

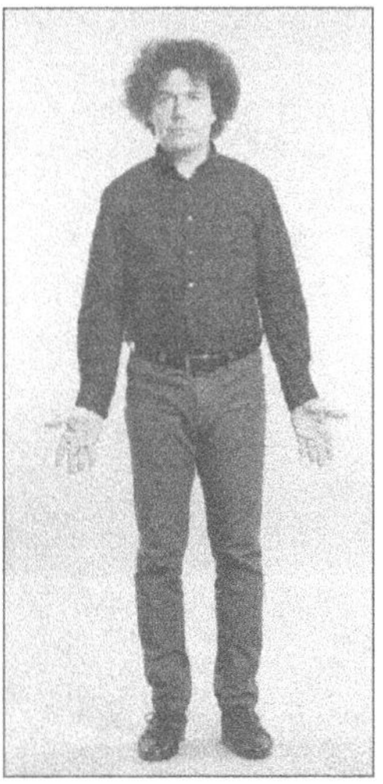
Figure 5b

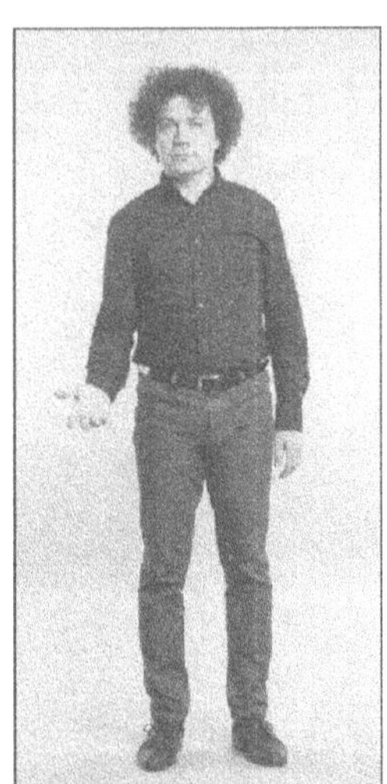
Figure 5c

Conclusion

The phrase in the gesture and in the look represents consecutive and meaningful gestures and looks which represent a complete thought. The most suitable level of gesticulation is between the height of the elbows and the chin of the performer. In this way the hands fall within the peripheral vision zone of the performers and the spectators and their eyes are not turned away from our eyes. The exceptions happen in cases when we put some accent, reach a culmination or use some choreography—then gestures need to be below the level of the elbows or above the level of the chin. In the first case the gestures become small and invisible, in the second—we hide our faces.

Chapter 8

Working with Lyrics

In this chapter we will look into working with lyrics from the moment we read them for the first time to the recording. We will elaborate on understanding the lyrics, defining the "strong" and "weak" words. We will discuss the lyrics as the starting point for the creation of the character we will present on stage. We will see how the song is split in parts by duration with the purpose of conquering the stage.

The phrase in the text, look and gesture will be covered. Having read this chapter, the "singing body" will be an ever more attainable goal for you!

Some pieces have been specially written for a voice but without a text:

Ella Fitzgerald, One Note Samba Scat Singing (https://www.youtube.com/watch?v=PbL9vr4Q2LU—active as of 23.02.2015);

Bobby McFerrin, My Favorite Things (https://www.youtube.com/watch?v=43Th4KleuBo—active as of 23.02.2015);

"Rodna Pessen" Choir "A Song without Words," music by Dimitar Konstantzaliev (https://www.youtube.com/watch?v=LeL1FDBN230—active as of 23.02.2015);

Stage Performance for Singers: A Practical Course in 12 Basic Steps
Martin Karnolsky

ISBN 978-981-4800-20-4 (Paperback), 978-0-429-42869-2 (eBook)
www.panstanford.com

"Badinera" J. S. Bach, Yildiz Ibrahimova (https://www.youtube.com/watch?v=ubf1im0v-uc—active as of 23.02.2015);

"Rondo a la Turka," W. A. Mozart (https://www.youtube.com/watch?v=0L3vcdzQPPU—active as of 23.02.2015);

"Sarabanda"—J.S.Bach, Aleksandar Chekmarev (https://www.youtube.com/watch?v=dPmTcEKt1s4—active as of 23.02.2015).

The majority of vocal pieces are composed of melody, lyrics and accompaniment. We will not discuss the variants of accompaniment, but we can say there are musical pieces which have no instrumental accompaniment—they have only a melody and lyrics (a cappella). In the case of others the accompaniment is vocal and is has lyrics like the solo part:

"Medley"—Take 6 (https://www.youtube.com/watch?v=QkL3nBCpoCo—active as of 23.02.2015);

Westminster Chorus—2010 International Chorus Champions (https://www.youtube.com/watch?v=67HtWxSWILg—active as of 23.02.2015).

See more at: www.martinkarnolsky.com

We will be looking into the basic principles of working with lyrics in a vocal piece.

When we hold for the first time the music and the lyrics of a new piece, we start by carefully reading the lyrics and listening to the melody and the accompaniment. Reading the lyrics for the very first time, we get an impression about many things—the subject, the mood, the complexity of words from the singing point of view, the juncture where we take "breaths" between words, etc.

After the first reading we should already have an idea on whether we like the lyrics or not. Whether it is right for us from the point of view of gender, age, social status, our preferred genre and so on. Irrespective of whether we perform the music or listen to it we establish the stage of completeness of the song. It may have been set only for the piano or the accompaniment may have already been prepared. Whatever the case, we have a clear picture of the style, genre, tempo, rhythm and other elements of the music. To put it differently: we analyze the piece and the lyrics, in particular. The analysis studies the smallest details, it depicts, examines, evaluates, acknowledges, rejects, confirms.

It defines the basic line of development and the thought (the super task and the all-pervading action of the piece and the role). The material feeds the imagination, the feeling, the thought and the will. It is not sufficient to say Stanislavsky offered a working model of behavior and attitude when we talk about the lyrics. Instead, he offers an algorithm towards solving the problem of lyric analysis. An algorithm offers clear guidance on solving a problem or a certain type of problem through a system of instructions. This algorithm of analysis and understanding the problems of the role was provided by Stanislavsky a long time ago. We need to note that the algorithm used for the analysis of the whole role in a theatrical piece of work does *not* differ from the algorithm used with small "etude" forms—the monologue, the song, the poem.

What are "strong" and "weak" words in the text? They may be strong or weak depending on the lyrics and the message we need to convey:

"I live in a house which is quite . . . big and beautiful."

"I live in a house which is quite . . . far down the road."

"I live in a house which is quite . . . valuable to me."

The text of the three examples is almost identical, so we must pay special attention to what exactly we want to stress. It is not only that text that we will play or sing. We must also look at the whole text for orientation.

Let us start with one sentence:

"I live in a house which is quite . . . big and beautiful."

If we agree we want to boast, the emphatic word will be "I." Normally, the gesture will point at ourselves.

"I live in a house which is quite . . . far down the road."

The emphasis in this sentence is my living in a house *far down* the road. This will be strengthened by the gesture.

"I live in a house which is quite . . . valuable to me."

In this instance, the dominant word is one which indicates our attitude to our home. However, every actor may choose another strong word which may be emphasized by a gesture.

Oh! Susanna
Original 1848

Music: Stephen Foster
Lyrics: Tom Roush

The song is occasionally (and incorrectly) called "Banjo on My Knee":

> I come from Alabama with a banjo on my knee,
> I'm going to Louisiana, my true love for to see
> It rained all night the day I left, the weather it was dry
> The sun so hot I froze to death; Susanna, don't you cry.
>
> Oh, Susanna, don't you cry for me
> cos' I come from Alabama
> With my banjo on my knee.
>
> I had a dream the other night when everything was still,
> I thought I saw Susanna coming up the hill,
> A buck wheat cake was in her mouth, a tear was in her eye,
> I said I'm coming from the south, Susanna don't you cry.
>
> I soon will be in New Orleans and then I'll look around
> And when I find my Susanna, I'll fall upon the ground
> But if I do not find her, this man will surely die
> And when I'm dead and buried, Susanna don't you cry.

We can examine these lyrics of a very popular song as follows: "What is he trying to tell us?" We begin by omitting the words which do not follow the general idea, and just makes beautiful poetry from a simple message. Here's the result if I had to sing this song and prepare for a stage performance:

> I come with a banjo,
> I'm going, my love for to see
> It rained, the weather it was dry
> The sun so hot I froze to death; Susanna, don't you cry.
>
> Oh, Susanna, don't you cry for me
> 'cos I come
> With my banjo.

I had a dream,
I thought I saw Susanna,
A cake was in her mouth, a tear was in her eye,
I said I'm coming, Susanna don't you cry.

I soon will be in New Orleans
When I find my Susanna, I'll fall upon the ground
If I do not find her, this man will die
And when I'm dead, Susanna don't you cry.

Well, what is left is far from poetry, but this is the main idea of the lyrics. Now you need to determine the *strong* and *weak* words. In fact, these are the words which we will enrich with information using our gestures. With so many remaining words, there is probably more than one option, right? This is my version:

I come with a banjo,
I'm going, *my love* for to see.
It rained, the weather it was dry,
The sun so hot *I froze* to death; *Susanna, don't you* cry.

Oh, *Susanna*, don't you cry for me
cos' *I come*
With *my* banjo.

I had *a dream*,
I thought *I saw Susanna*,
A cake was in her mouth, *a tear* was in her eye,
I said I'm *coming*, Susanna *don't you cry*.

Oh, Susanna, *don't you cry* for me
cos' *I come*
With my *banjo*

I soon will be in New Orleans.
When I find *my Susanna, I'll fall* upon the ground
If I do not find her, this man *will die*
And when *I'm dead, Susanna* don't you cry.

Oh, *Susanna*, don't you cry *for me*
cos' *I* come
With my banjo.

Note that the bold words can mislead you to repeat them literally with a gesture. Also note that when the chorus is repeated, I am looking for different strong words. If we don't want our performance to resemble that of kindergarten kids, it should include a variety of gestures, glances, and moves on the stage. I know that everyone understands that it is much more difficult to explain the above on paper than to actually demonstrate it. However, I hope that everyone gets the main idea—we emphasize what we consider to be strong words and use a variety of gestures. If we need to repeat a part of the lyrics in the song, we can skip some of the gestures. This also creates the impression of diversity in the gestures.

I draw your attention to the following: when we sing some lyrics, we have to understand them to the very last syllable! This means that we sing in a language we understand or have learnt the lyrics so well that it does not show we don't understand the language. Very often we can see and hear singers who are simply singing in a foreign language. It will *always* show if you do not understand the lyrics! Even more so if the performers are artistic and know what to do on stage but feel like their hands are tied as they do not understand the lyrics in detail.

You cannot enrich the lyrics with a gesture if you do not know what they are about and what the specific word means!

If we have reviewed the lyrics and have learnt them to the very last syllable, we are ready to create the character to be presented to the audience. The lyrics are the starting point. We have to understand the character and round him or her off with content. There is the costume which comes next—we will discuss that later. We continue with how we will look on the stage in general and our actions on the stage. Will there be any special choreography movements, dancing or something similar? Having taken the final decision on how the song will be presented, we start working on it. We rehearse the singing, the mise-en-scene, the look, the gestures. We rehearse everything! During rehearsal, we may stumble on some interesting ideas or discover things not suitable for presentation. Everything must be rehearsed!

It is important that we decide on the split of the song by stage space at the rehearsal stage. Having read the lyrics and the music you now know the number of couplets. The character is created, so it is time to think about how much space we need and how to use it. Will we be standing in the center of the stage all the time? Or will we make our entry during the introduction of the song? Will we start singing at the back of the stage or from one side? Should we move to the left and to the right and how many times do we need to do that to communicate with the audience? The song needs to be clearly split in parts, depending on its form and duration. This is a simple mechanical activity but it has to be planned. For example: the first couplet and the refrain—in the center of the stage. The second couplet—on the left side. The refrain—in the center. The third couplet—on the right side. The last refrain—in the center. This is also where we bow. This is a simple scheme but it may be different for the very same song. It is important that the duration and the form of the song are distributed in a way that will leave time for everything we have planned to do to send the message to the audience. It is the lyrics that contain the specific information in a vocal piece, so we need to know that the phrase, the gesture and the look will be defined by the general idea of the lyrics. I want to emphasize that it is all guided by the lyrics. This may have become clear when we elaborated on the phrase in the text. There is nothing scary about it! We just follow the lyrics! The definition will be the same. A complete sequence of gestures, looks and words which compose a phrase, the latter being suitable to be separated from the whole text.

Having learnt and done all the above we begin the preparation for the sound recording. Many believe that this is a very simple process. In fact, the sound recording is the most difficult part of the singer's work. The difficulty comes from the need to make the recording interesting enough to be listened to. It needs to be impressive in itself without any feedback fron the audience. Anyone who has visited a sound studio knows that it is a soundproof room, very often without windows. You can see nothing but the sound engineer. He is in an adjacent room and we can hear him on the headphones or monitors. In some studios the sound engineer is a sort of an "imaginary" figure as we have no visual contact with him. We can just hear him. What is important is that there is nobody to inspire us while we are recording. I have always advised musicians to enter the studio well prepared. We need to know the score so well as to be able to start playing or singing it from almost any note. As we have no feedback from the audience, we need to have mastered the character so well that we can sing as if in a huge stadium crammed with a hundred thousand people watching and listening to us. This is why I stressed that the sound recording stage is the most difficult part of the singer's work. It is not singing in tune, but the pretended mood that is the most difficult to master in the studio.

Let us return to the lyrics. While reading and thinking over a particular song, we need to know of vocal artistry. There are certain practices which we will discuss in the following chapter. But when we enter the studio we should already know the range and limits of the voice and its entry into artistic dimensions. Every breath and tone will be already thought through, taken up and rehearsed in a way which will allow the song to be sung twice in the very same manner. In the past, even until the beginning of the 90s a certain technique of recording was very popular in some countries. The solo part was recorded twice—i.e., it was dubbed. The goal of this technique was to collect more "colors" in the singer's timbre. I hope you understand what I mean! Every tone, syllable and breath must be learnt in the rehearsal hall in order to be able to repeat the same thing twice! Even if you do not dub your solo part, you must know the song you want to record perfectly!

Conclusion

To sum it up: we read the lyrics carefully and listen to the music with the purpose of defining the character of the role. We look for difficult melody "leaps" or sequences, as well as for words which are difficult to pronounce and sing. We look for adjacent "explosive" consonants and any other traps which can make the performance harder. We seek to probe the lyrics deeply so that we know what is behind the words. In this way the gestures will come naturally and enrich the meaning. Singing in a foreign language does not mean we should understand *every* word in the text. The selection of the "strong" and "weak" words is important to add gestures to specific words. Usually, it is to the "strong" words that we add gestures. The lyrics, which are our basic source of specific information, are the starting point for the creation of the stage character for a given song. The exceptions are pieces written for voice only. In this case the character will depend on the genre, style, epoch and all other information which may help to define it. When everything has been read and clarified, we split the lyrics so we have enough time to walk over the whole stage, to communicate and finish the performance at the center of the stage.

The phrase in the text, look and gesture: A complete sequence of gestures, looks and words, which constitute a phrase, the latter being suitable to be separated from the whole text.

The sound recording, being the most difficult part of the singer's work, must be prepared to such exacting standards that it allows the whole piece to be repeated twice in the very same way. Thus we can be certain that we will be able to record the piece or song in parts, the final result being one in which no emotion, feeling, voice features, and artistry will be lost. To put it in other words, the listener should have the impression that it has been sung in one piece, as we sing at a concert and will not be able to tell the difference due to the dubbing!

Chapter 9

Artistry in the Voice

In this chapter we will answer the question what artistry in the voice is. We will elaborate on some practices which profit by artistry. We will also talk about overacting.

What is artistry in the voice? This is the total of all practices, used by the performer with the purpose of recreating and suggesting to the audience his desired thoughts, images, situation, using only his voice. These include singing, speaking, filler sounds, munching, shouts, etc. One of the strongest instruments of the singer is his artistry in the voice. It must be able to laugh, weep, rejoice, suffer, shout and pray in different situations. It can slow down in order to tell us something. It may switch on to a recitative, to whispering or to very loud breathing when necessary. To sigh, not to breathe. All these and many more represent artistry in the voice! Having mentioned some of the practices used by singers to convey and suggest the message of the song to the audience, we also have to remember not to overdo it. This is also called overacting. This occurs when gestures, facial expressions, the voice and other practices are used too much and the general feeling conveyed is of the character being artificial. There is always a *but*, however. Overacting may be a practice which may suggest something. Imagine that the performance includes the character

Stage Performance for Singers: A Practical Course in 12 Basic Steps
Martin Karnolsky

ISBN 978-981-4800-20-4 (Paperback), 978-0-429-42869-2 (eBook)
www.panstanford.com

of a clown, a Charlie Chaplin or involves parody sketch elements. Then, overacting can be a credible method. And we can conclude that the technical and creative instruments have been used to perfection. But we also need a *sense of proportion*! This sense will let us know whether we have got it right and in a credible manner. This is why overacting and a lack of stage presence in themselves simply cannot be called *good performances*!

Conclusion

What is artistry in the voice? This is the total of all practices, used by the performer with the purpose of recreating and suggesting to the audience his desired thoughts, images, situation, using only his voice. It is one of his strongest instruments. Artistry may easily transform into overacting, but overacting itself may also be used.

Chapter 10

The Costume

In this chapter we will define the concept of costume. We will try to "put on" a costume and learn about the pluses and minuses of its use. We will explain why it is useful to rehearse with the costume on. We will look into how far fantasy may go regarding costume preparation. Finally, we will discuss some of the most showy of "artistic" costumes.

The costume is the collection of clothes, shoes, makeup, jewellery, hairstyles, accessories, objects and everything else that can be part of the function of the stage attire that can add to the character and make it more outstanding. The stage costume (costume in French and Italian means 'custom') is one of the most important components of a performance. It is used by the actor to display the characteristic features of the stage character, and is designed on the basis of the director's idea. Makeup and hairstyle are necessary additions to the costume.

The costume is an independent part of the creative work of the stage actor—in it he creates the world of images—social, satirical, grotesque, tragic, fairy tales and others.

In general, the costume is the first thing the spectator sees. It is the costume that creates the first impression on the audience about us. I have mentioned that the first impression about a person

Stage Performance for Singers: A Practical Course in 12 Basic Steps
Martin Karnolsky

ISBN 978-981-4800-20-4 (Paperback), 978-0-429-42869-2 (eBook)
www.panstanford.com

is formed during the first 90 seconds. By this time up to 95% of the impression is formed. The remaining 5% will be formed during the following hours, days, weeks, sometimes months. What I mean is that when we step out on stage the costume must be able to attract the attention of the audience and convey the right impression on the nature of our performance. As the audience is at a certain distance from the performer, the small elements need to be carefully considered. Quite often there will be nothing particular about the costume—it may be a beautiful dress, a pair of modern trousers and a shirt, a short sleeves blouse, a stylish suit. But again: quite often the character may require a special attitude to the costume. We may have to portray an epoch, a profession, represent a mythical or ordinary animal. Sometimes some objects, the weather or geographical concepts may be our "costume." It is all dependent on the lyrics which contain the specific information and which set the starting point of the stage performance. But it does also depend on our creative interpretation of the character. Some characters may be presented by a dance or a mise-en-scene and that will spare putting on costumes of unusual form and color which will need time and money to create.

What does the costume give us and what does it take from us? In a joint concert we very often do not have the time to change costumes during our participation of 15 or 20 minutes. Even if we have more time, it is better to wear a costume which will be convenient for our whole program. That means that specific costumes—the jester's or the hunter's will not be suitable. There is no time to change costumes. Apart from the case when by taking off a part of the costume, a new one appears. This may be used for songs for which special costumes are necessary. If this is not the case, then we can count on a shawl, a wig, a hat, a walking stick and other accessories which will very quickly transform the appearance of the character. These are elements which will instantly show what the character we now represent is.

These are issues which, if solved, can grant us bigger success. What should the costume be? First, it must be *comfortable*! It is most important that we feel at ease and are not disturbed by what we have put on, carry in our hands or on our heads. The fabric must not make us hot or cold while on stage. Our movements must not be hindered by it. All that must be taken into consideration while inventing the character. Quite often, not much attention is paid to shoes, but they are as important as the other components of the costume. They also need to be comfortable.

Let us note here that some stages echo when we walk on them. They may be hollow below the wooden floor. This is why we need to wear shoes with soft soles so that no distracting sounds are produced. When we are on stage for an hour and a half, it is *obligatory* that the shoes are comfortable. Our feet should not hurt because we have been standing or dancing on the stage. Having defined the character we will portray, we need to rehearse with the costume on. If the costume is a special one, this is important. Imagine the costume of a musketeer. A rapier, a pistol, a wide-brimmed hat with a feather. These are all specific parts of the costume which you need to master. If your role demands fencing skills with your rapier, you need to rehearse the actions. Getting a rapier out can be awkward as also putting it back in its sheath. You need to practice these movements. You also need to practice how to take your hat off and how to curtsy. You cannot imagine what could become an obstacle. Also, we have not mentioned yet that you may have the mike in your hand—one more aspect to consider. It is good to have mirrors in the rehearsal hall. Mirrors are of exceptional importance for the actor's work. Both mirrors and video recordings are our friends. They show us all the mistakes and spare us nothing. We need to be able to see our mistakes and understand them. Then find a way to correct them.

Here are some of the most striking costumes of modern show business worn by Lady Gaga, Madonna, Robin Williams, Kiss and others.

Examples

https://www.youtube.com/watch?v=NH765PXfFwg

http://moviepilot.com/posts/3544955

http://www.cosmopolitan.co.uk/fashion/celebrity/news/a38329/lady-gagas-meat-dresswhat-looks-like-now-photos/

http://www.yellmagazine.com/everything-i-know-about-sex-i-learned-fromkiss/72090/#

http://front.bg/razvlechenija/lubopitno/spreli-zdravnite-osigurovki-na-azis

https://itgirlguide.bg/2016/03/22/%D0%B0%D0%B7%D0%B8%D1%81-%D0%BF%D1%80%D0%B5%D0%B2%D0%B7%D0%B5-%D0%B1%D1%80%D0%BE%D0%B4%D1%83%D0%B5%D0%B9/

http://www.theguardian.com/music/2014/nov/06/queen-forever-review-compilation

https://www.farnazfever.com/article/freddie-mercury-story-behind-true-rock-%E2%80%98n%E2%80%99-roll-legend

http://www.kamerado.nl/marillion-fish.html

See more at: www.martinkarnolsky.com

Conclusion

The costume is the collection of clothes, makeup, hairstyles, accessories, objects and everything else that can be part of the function of the stage attire that can add to the character and make it more outstanding.

The costume may help us portray the character, but could also cause physical difficulties during the performance. It may complicate the overall presentation if it is part of a big concert and there is no time to change costumes between songs. Rehearsing with the costume on is obligatory! We must get used to the costume. Or get accustomed to this "new skin" so that we look natural on stage. The costume must not be a hindrance or make us sweat or shiver. Shoes must be comfortable and soft, aiding easy and fluid movement on stage without emitting unnecessary and distracting sounds.

Chapter 11

Makeup and Hairstyle

In this chapter we will discuss makeup and hairstyles as part of the character in general, emphasizing the importance of these elements both on and off stage. Plus we will expound on the variety of makeup and hairstyles.

It is inevitable that makeup and hairstyle be vital components in our presentation. Starting with the fact that we need to look just right from the esthetical point of view. Let us return to stage presentation.

The makeup and hairdo may drastically change our appearance. They may make us unrecognizable. Again, we have to be careful. There are hairstyles and makeup which are not suitable for all ages, styles, genres, gender, height, etc. An example: quite often we cannot compare the height of the performer to that of another. If we are sure that the person is above 16 or 18, things will be easier. However, in the case of children, it may become interesting. On stage we may have a woman in an evening dress, with a hairstyle suitable for a five-star restaurant or a visit to the Bolshoi Theater. The makeup may correspond to what is called evening makeup. But after the concert you see an ordinary 10- or 12-year-old girl, not taller than 130 cm. Now this comes as a shock.

Stage Performance for Singers: A Practical Course in 12 Basic Steps
Martin Karnolsky

ISBN 978-981-4800-20-4 (Paperback), 978-0-429-42869-2 (eBook)
www.panstanford.com

Referring again to the moment of selecting the repertoire, we need to stress that the selection is coupled by the actions which follow. These include the choice of character, costume, hairstyle, makeup, behavior, etc. The appearance of the performer may contradict what suits him. This is why the hairstyle and the makeup must correspond to his age. Further, we need to consider the two types of makeup—stage makeup and society makeup. There are some peculiarities inherent to the stage and these cannot be neglected. For example, there may be photo and video cameras at work. The lights may be very powerful. If we need the makeup to be visible from afar, it has to be expressive and expertly done. It may also be invisible—the tones on the face may be made equal, we may want to conceal or emphasize a certain facet. Beads of sweat must not be seen. If it is too hot, we must make sure the countenance is not shiny. The hairstyle must not hide the face and hinder our artistic performance. It must correspond to the age, gender, height and weight, among other characteristics. But what is vital is that the the hairstyle must suit the general demeanour, the general idea of the character being portrayed. I would like to point to something exceptionally important and true.

On the stage the actors demonstrate fashion trends similar to models. They may sometimes launch them. At times we may perceive imitations of a preferred singer or actor manifested in the behavior, clothes, the hairstyle or the makeup. The actors on stage have an educational role to play! They must be one step ahead of the spectators. They *have the right* to be more extravagant. They may be dressed in a kitsch, impractical or strange manner. But they *have no right* to look ordinary. Every actor must know this: always find a way to step on stage in a costume different from your day to day clothes. This involves unconscious self-preparation. You need to be fully prepared for your audience! What I want to say, finally, is that how we look is of great importance. It is important for the stage, and no less so off stage. Use a simple guiding principle: always be ready for a TV interview! This will make you take care of your appearance so that you are always prepared should photo or video cameras appear.

Conclusion

The makeup and hairstyle represent important elements of the stage character. They may show an epoch, a profession, a state of mind. They must conform to the age, height, weight, physical features, costume, etc. The actor must always be one step ahead of the spectator, including with his hairdo and makeup. Also, off stage we must always look ready for a TV interview.

Chapter 12

The Bow and Leaving the Stage

In this chapter we will examine the bow and the types of bows. We will clarify on how to brow and on how close to the ground. We will learn how to control the audience by bowing and about leaving the stage in a manner inoffensive to the audience.

Bowing to the ground is almost universally used as a sign of subservience, of respect or humility when we feel honored, like in the case of ovations. Note how the Japanese (and the Chinese to a lesser degree) bow as a sign of respect and reverence. When we automatically bow to the waist or to the ground, we show that we are subordinates or have a lower stature. Bows are made by bending the torso. Western people will not easily bow to the ground, in particular when this is a conscious act. With widening horizons and increased communication with people, for the Near East and the Far East it becomes necessary to learn to bend our torso, in particular, when we meet elderly people who deserve respect. This simple gesture of respect will be noted by those whose culture expresses respect with a similar pose and will be a social advantage to Westerners who would like to demonstrate it. By the way, in Eastern Europe older people will still put their heels together and bow slightly as a sign of respect. Every time

Stage Performance for Singers: A Practical Course in 12 Basic Steps
Martin Karnolsky

ISBN 978-981-4800-20-4 (Paperback), 978-0-429-42869-2 (eBook)
www.panstanford.com

I see this I cannot but think how charming it is that people can still show politeness and reverence in the contemporary world. Done consciously or unconsciously, the bow is a non-verbal gesture of respect for others (Joe Navarro and Marvin Karlins, *What Every BODY is Saying: An Ex-FBI Agent's Guide to Speed-Reading People*).

"The bow is a non-verbal gesture of respect for others." This is a very general definition of the term bow. I would suggest a definition of my own, directed at the activities of the singer and actor and which incorporates the first definition: "The bow is part of the song and the natural closing of our performance by means of which we show our respect and gratitude to the audience." This is our last action on the stage prior to leaving it. This is what leaves the final impression on the audience. The very final action is, actually, leaving the stage, but it is a part of the bow and the whole performance.

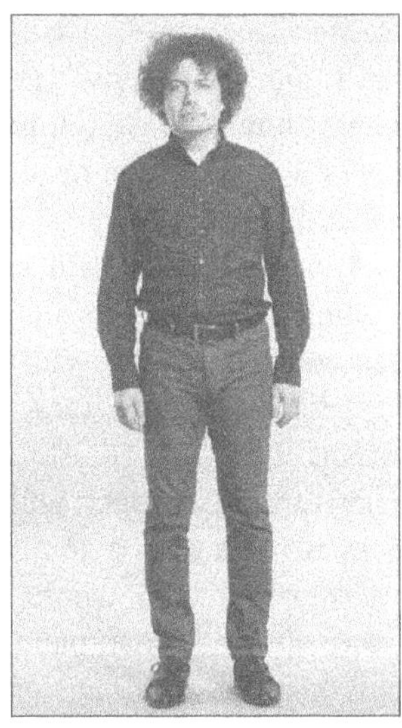

Figure 1

By claiming that the bow is part of the song I mean that you cannot walk on to the stage in a ball gown, sing about princes and princesses, send the audience into ecstacy with your performance and then just nod your head. Or turn around and run out of the stage like Cinderella when the clock strikes 12 and the magic disappears. *Remember*: the bow is part of the song! If you portray a princess, your bow will be composed but very lady-like and gentle. Queens, princesses, kings, princes, the military and the winners in tournaments and competitions do not bow (Fig. 1). But a musketeer standing in front of a gorgeous lady will take down his hat and bow to the ground (Fig. 2).

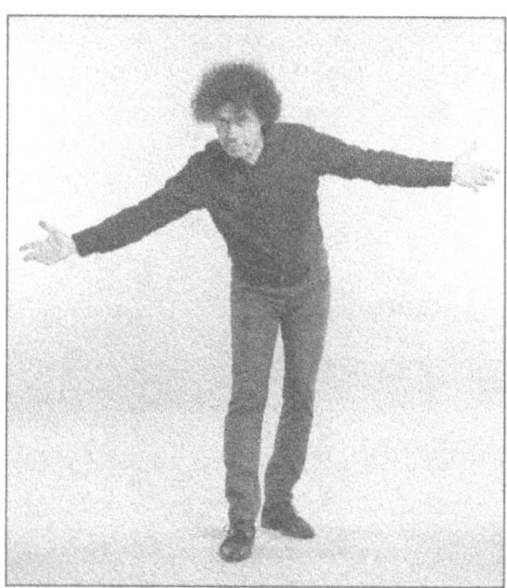

Figure 2

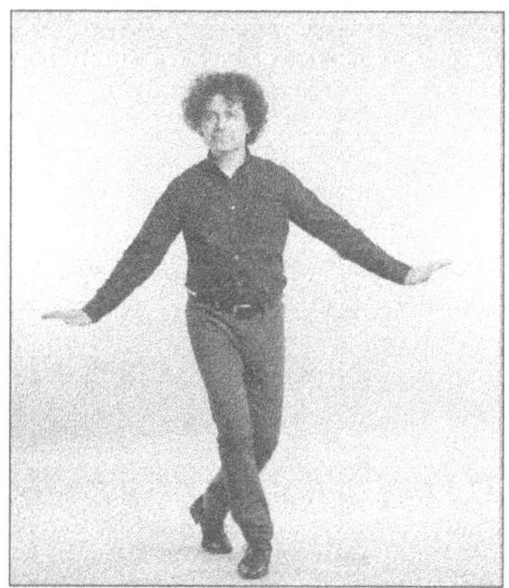

Figure 3

If we are referring to the character of a little girl, she will make a low curtsey (Fig. 3). Gentlemen may also take off their hats and bow (Fig. 4). Let us not forget that the bow is part of the song and it will depend on the character we portray on the stage. The gentleman or the musketeer may not be part of the "good" characters. Their bows will not be "good." If your role is of a soldier or a marine—salute (Fig. 5). Or you may take off your hat and nod energetically. All that is based on the lyrics. The story gives us the whole information. What remains is a matter of interpretation on our behalf.

We have partially mentioned the types of bows. They may be split by several features. The first two—group and individual ones. The group bows are used when we have ensemble performances—choirs, duos, trios and other chamber formations. The folklore ensembles are a clear example of that (Fig. 6).

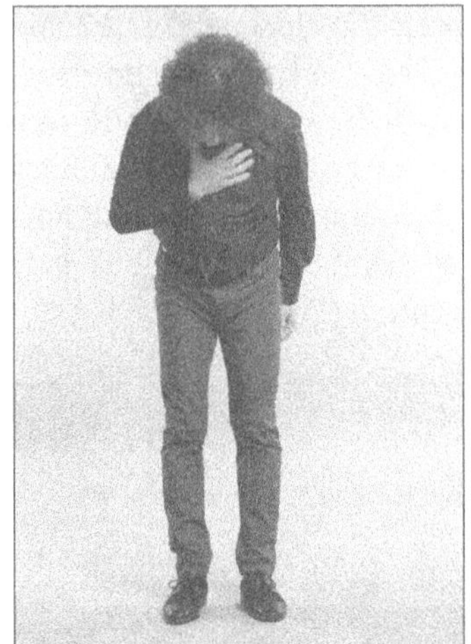

Figure 4

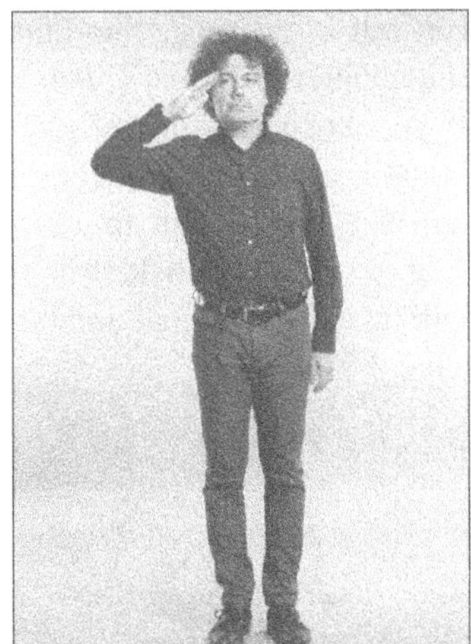

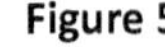

Figure 5

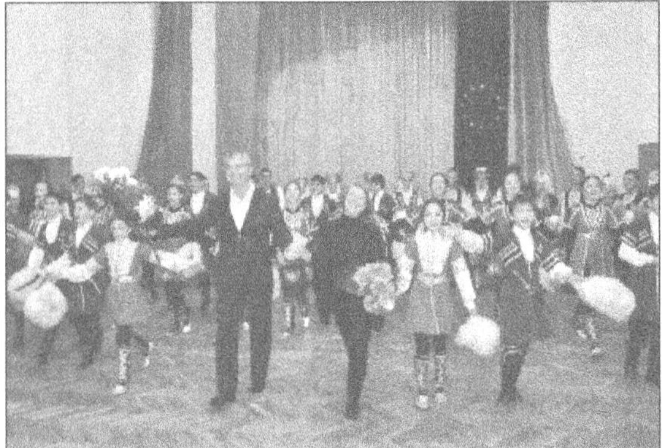

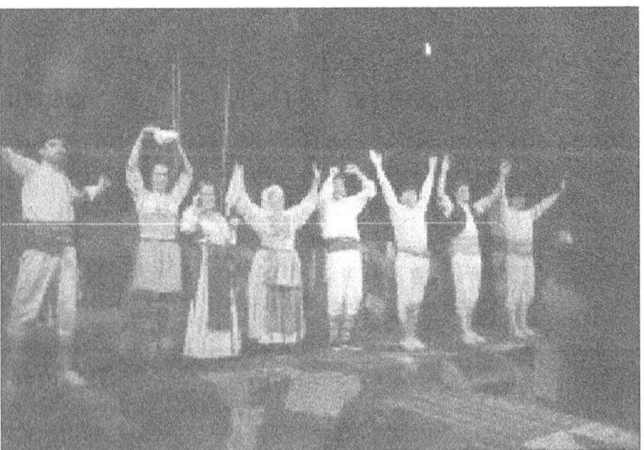

Figure 6

It is also very interesting to watch the theatre bows. In this case the bow is part of the whole performance. The actors still play their roles, they bow individually, in couples, in groups of characters and according to the significance of the characters. At the end they also bow together.

Examples

https://www.youtube.com/watch?v=8K1G93lierQ

https://svejo.net/stories/1697902-fevruari-2013-vzriv-skandali-i-edin-golyam-poklon

https://www.miloserdie.ru/article/upsala-cirk-sovremennaya-pedagogicheskaya-poema/

https://www.bilettorg.ru/shows/132/

See more at: www.martinkarnolsky.com

The individual bows are clear to define—the performer is alone on stage and he is not bowing in a group.

Depending on how we bow, we differentiate between two groups too: big (Fig. 7) and small bows (Fig. 8).

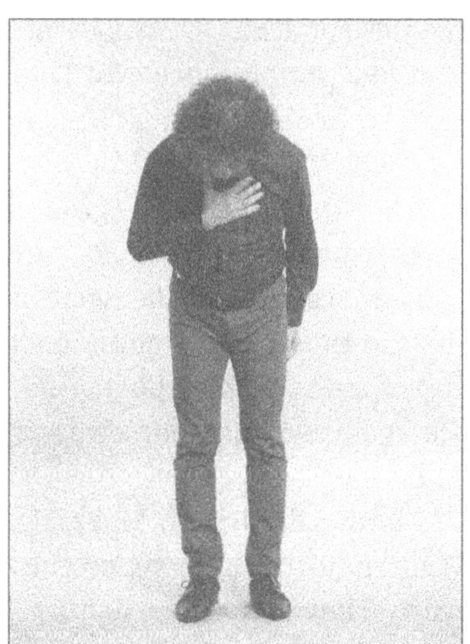

Figure 7

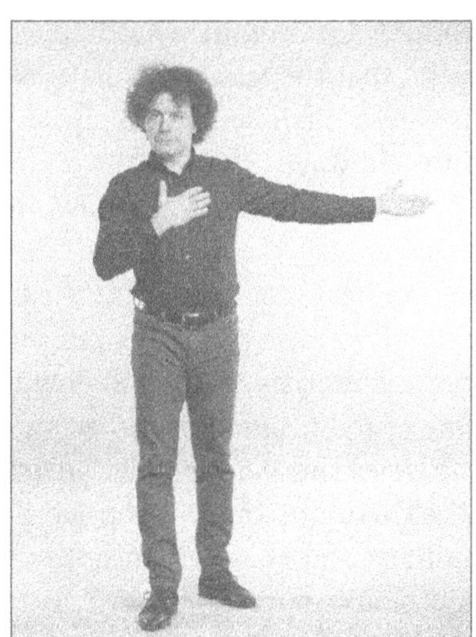

Figure 8

With the big bow the body bends up to 90 degrees and we lose visual contact with the audience or the object of the bowing.

This is historically predetermined. As mentioned above, kings do not bow. Neither do soldiers. But subordinates bow *to the ground*. Looking down at the floor or the ground, we acknowledge that we face someone or a group of people who stand higher in the hierarchy. We must not mistake the bow for the traditional greeting of the East. We mentioned that when talking about the gesture. We need to know the customs of the people for whom we perform. It is not only the gestures which we make with our hands, but also the behavior of the body and eyes that are not acceptable to some peoples. At the outset, we need to be the first to greet an elderly Japanese with a bow and restore our upright position prior to his greeting. And, finally, if we have been granted an audience with kings or presidents, we can do nothing before receiving the acknowledgement of the high ranked host. This does not mean that our dignity may suffer. Again, we need to know the customs of the audience and take all specific aspects into consideration.

I now make a small digression related to the bow. In the Far East clapping your hands and demonstrating the inner emotional state of the audience is by no means customary. What we are accustomed to at concerts in Europe and North America has nothing to do with what happens in the Far East! This does not mean that the spectators have disliked our performance. No! They manifest their emotions in a more reserved manner and in different ways.

Let us return to the bow. Apart from the bow to the ground there is also the small one. This is what princes, princesses and the military do—they nod their heads energetically. The same is true of winners in battle, but only before those who stand higher in the hierarchy. The small bow is that of men. We may bow in this way without being in the army. Once again we base ourselves on the lyrics and the character we present.

There are cases when we do not bow. Like I said, kings, the military and winners do not bow. They hold their heads proudly and look opponents in their eyes. They are the winners! ("Полетели" ("Poleteli"), Philipp Kirkorov—https://www.youtube.com/watch?v=bUx2EaTSU04—active as of 11.12.2014).

In some musical genres the bow is not the most popular thing.

Examples

As a whole, rock singers are rebels and bowing is not part of their routine.

https://www.youtube.com/watch?v=EPHJFnob8p8

Rappers avoid bows. They are "bad" boys and girls and they cannot be commanded and managed. They are free!

http://getchorus.com/a-guide-to-getting-better-paying-rap-gigs/

http://www.vespermagazine.com/blog/2013/02/25/musiciens-je-veux-frencher-a-koriass-kickto-the-ovaries/

http://www.wallpaperup.com/tags/show/rapper

See more at: www.martinkarnolsky.com

We can identify other types of bows. What is important, however, is to understand the meaning of this action. The meaning is to give the audience their seconds or minutes when they feel part of our performance by applauding us. The audience have come with the purpose of listening and seeing something. They have come of their own free will. They have come to enjoy themselves. So we must give them the time and the opportunity to do so. If we nod quickly and run off the stage, the audience will be deeply disappointed with us. We take away their right to show their opinion on our performance. We deprive them of the pleasure to be part of the show. We thwart that natural moment of taking their breath between two performances by cutting down the time they need. This short time is needed for the audience to see us off and get tuned to the end of our performance and the beginning of the next. *Do not hurry*! Listen to how the audience applauds you and bow as long as is necessary. This may even bring an encore for you!

No servility is needed. We need not show unnecessarily that the audience is the "master." We need to respect both ourselves and the audience. Imagine you are in the course of a natural conversation with the audience. It needs to close in a natural manner. If, on the other hand, the conversation is this: "Listen! I have no time. Hurry up and bring me the car keys. Be quick! I am late!" and the answer to that is "OK, I am going!," then the separation of the two people in the conversation will be very short and without formalities. There is no time to be lost. But if you have been telling a long and interesting story, it is expected that your company would like to state their opinion. They may want to admire it, to show indignation or something else. You must give them time. *Do not hurry*! The tempo of your bow must allow the audience time to enjoy the performance and applaud. The bow should be *part of the song*! By its manner, duration and everything else.

How can we "manage" the spectators by means of the bow?

In general, it would be rather late if we rely only on the bow to get a call for an encore from the audience. For the purpose of the example we will agree that the performance has done its job—the audience liked us a lot. What remains to be done is bow and leave the stage. But there is a small secret which may make the audience applaud a second time. There may even be an encore call—maybe one small step or a last gesture has been missing to change the balance and sing an encore. Let us imagine you have a ball gown on and the song corresponds to your appearance. What remains to be done is bow. We bend down to 90 degrees. The hands are spread in a pose like an aircraft and we are looking to the ground in front of ourselves (Fig. 9).

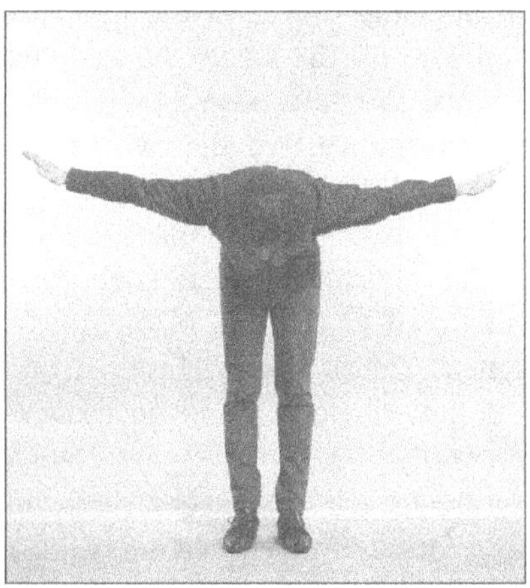

Figure 9

We stay like that and . . . wait! We wait and listen. We listen to the applause. When it starts dying out, we stand up. Then you will most probably hear how it quiets down very quickly. However, you are the star! Bow once again, but bend only to 45 degrees. Smile widely and look the audience in the eye (Figs. 10a–c).

The only thing guaranteed is renewed applause from the audience. This is guaranteed. But it is not certain there may be an encore—this depends on many other factors.

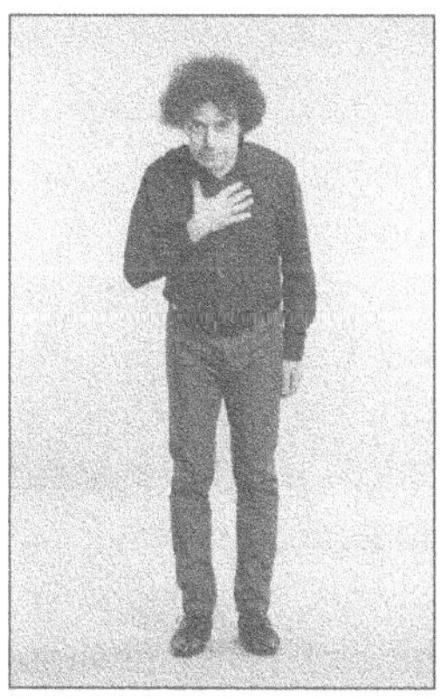
Figure 10a

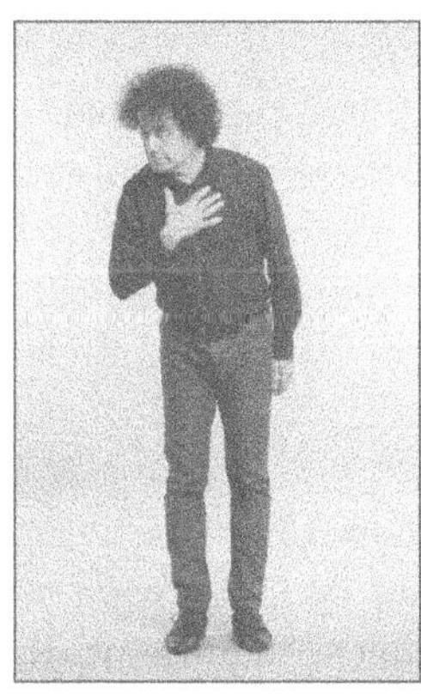
Figure 10b

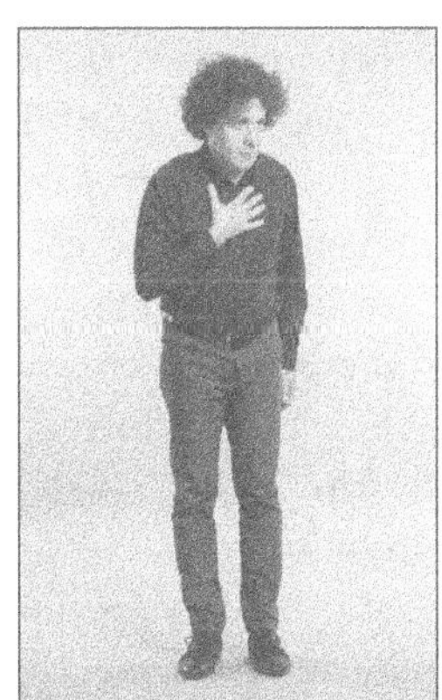
Figure 10c

However, with the second bow and by looking directly into the eyes of the people you will trigger new applause and will make the audience believe it *likes* you! I would like to make sure you understand: this is a *scheme*. It is no panacea, it is a general approach. If you play the role of a musketeer—the first bow will be deep to the ground, your hat will be off and your leg moved to the front (Fig. 11).

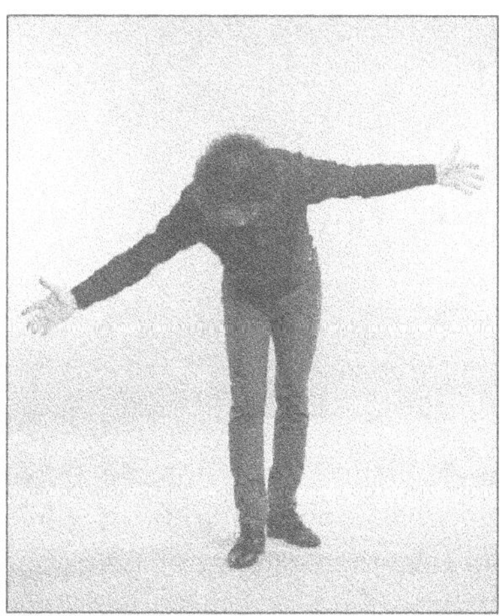
Figure 11

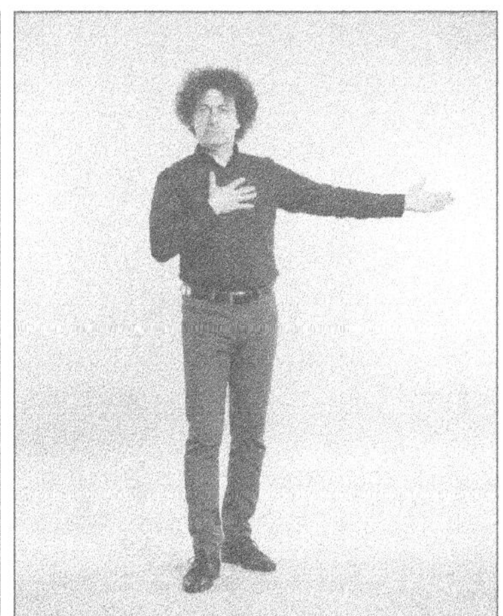
Figure 12

The second bow will not be that pronounced, your eyes will look down, your head will be lowered but much less than before—you need to see the eyes of the audience (Fig. 12). You react in a different way to each situation! Think separately about every song and every bow!

We have bowed. What comes next? We leave the stage to allow the other participants in the program to go on stage and present themselves to the audience. How do we do this? It is simple: the volume of the movements will differ depending on the dimensions of the stage. Otherwise, in general, things are similar. When the performance is over and we must leave from the side of the front stage, it is very easy. We turn in the desired direction and, showing one shoulder to the audience, we walk out (Fig. 13). We do not hurry if the song performed was slow. We may hurry if the character requires it. If the exit is somewhere at the rear we take *at least one step back*! Depending on the dimensions of the stage, the steps may be two or three. Only after that will we turn and show our backs to the audience (Figs. 14a and b).

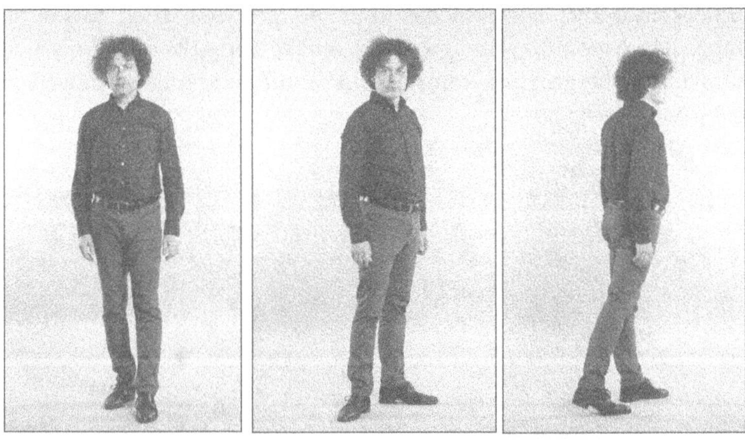

Figure 13 **Figure 14a** **Figure 14b**

If the stage is large and the applause does not die down quickly, you can use the space and make one or two bows while stepping back (Fig. 15a and b). You take the first one or two steps and bow. Then you repeat this, turn around and leave the stage

(Figs. 16a–c). You assess that on the spot. It depends on the applause, on the dimensions of the stage, on the tempo of the spectacle and many other aspects. What is important is that you do not turn your back to the audience and run away like someone who has been stealing cherries from the neighbor's orchard!

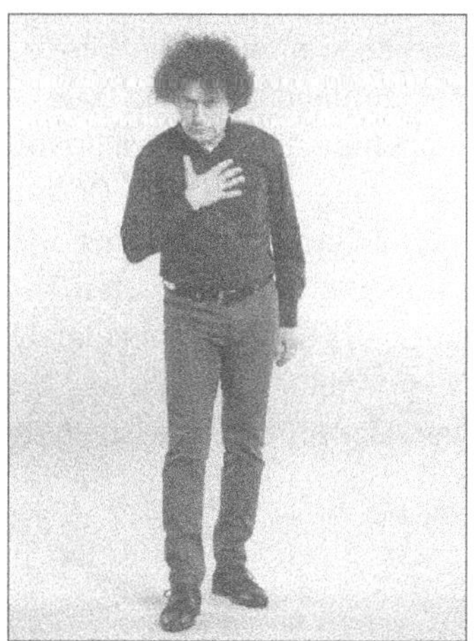

Figure 15a

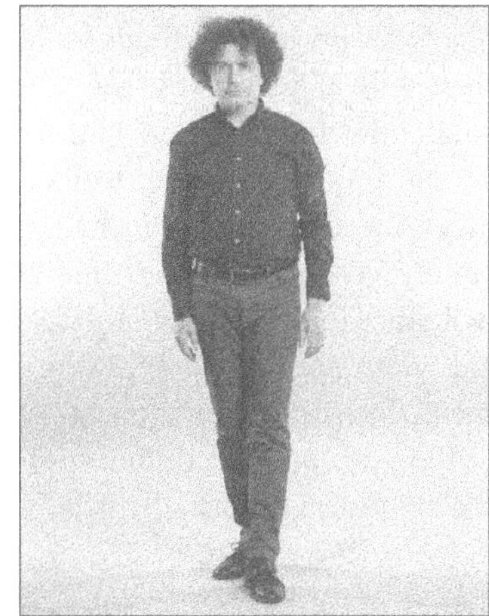

Figure 15b

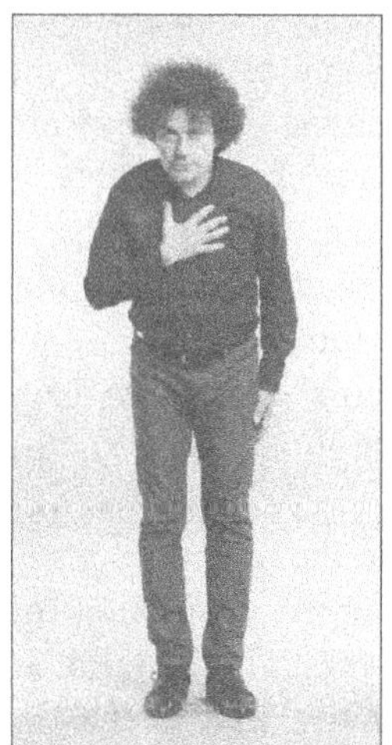

Figure 16a

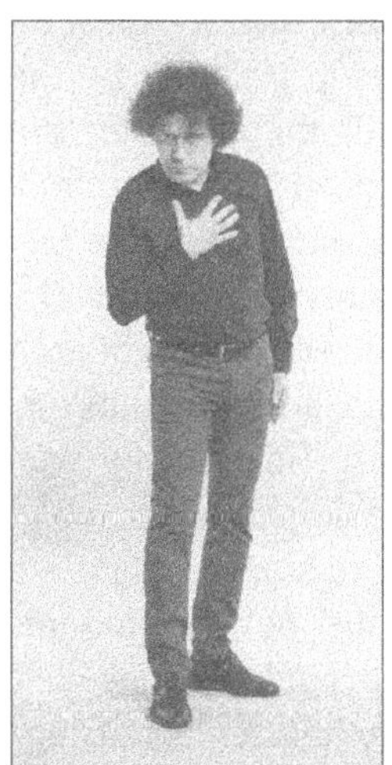

Figure 16b

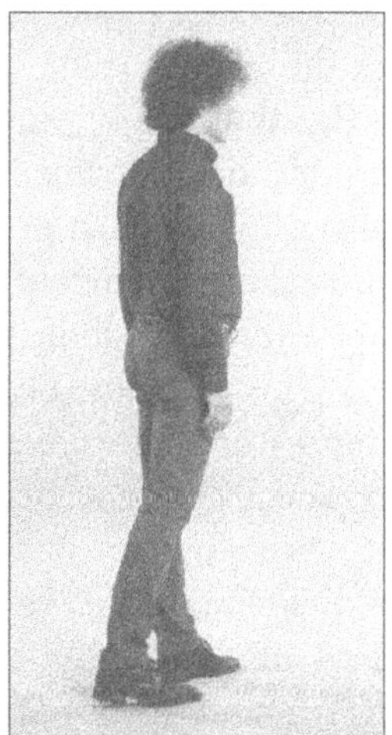

Figure 16c

Think about the bow and moving off the stage as of a separation with the interlocutors after a pleasant conversation. There may always be something more to say. There may always be something more to agree on. Do not hurry! Be the natural interlocutor of your audience.

There is one more option to consider. If you bow between songs, give the audience a moment to take their breath. The bow needs to be long enough to let the audience applaud as long as they will. If you think they should not applaud too long, take a small bow and stand upright. Then a short moment to take a breath should follow. A moment of silence—several seconds only. Or you may say something to change the sound background. This will simply give you a little time to tune into the next character. You will start telling a new story. You cannot start talking immediately. Let your spectators "chew over" the previous information. Let them tune in to your new story. And you already know what to do at the end: take a minimum of one step backwards before leaving the stage and that is all!

Conclusion

Bowing is part of the song and the natural closing of our performance by means of which we show our respect and gratitude to the audience. Its features should be the same as those of the song, thus being part of the character portrayed. The bows are group and individual, deep to the ground and shorter. There is also a form which does not necessitate bending the body—this is the manner winners and royals bow. The head stands proudly upright and the look is directed straight at the audience.

The duration of the bow depends on how deeply we have impressed the audience. This is why we carefully listen to the applause and react accordingly.

We must not hurry to stand upright while the applause is still at the climax. But we must not wait too long in the position of the bow or even after the applause has died out. The bow is an instrument we need to master. By using it, we may make the audience applaud a second time and even call for an encore. Having bowed, we must leave the stage. We do that by taking at least one step backwards without turning around or losing eye contact with the audience. The above is true in cases where the exit is at the rear of the stage and turning your back to the audience is inevitable. The steps may be more than one if the stage is a large one.

Exercises

The exercises which I will present to you are of two types. The first ones are for preparation before a stage performance. As we know, the body must be prepared for the forthcoming pressure. We warm up our voice prior to singing. When we work out we warm up the muscles. The same approach is valid here as well. We must prepare the limbs, the face and the body for what is coming. Also, at the end of the classes we relax the body, we discontinue the creative process both physically and psychologically. The second type of exercises are directly related to the stage performance training and refer to principles, methods, manner of thinking, etc. These assist the singer to teach his body to "sing" together with him. They help develop the capacity of communicating with the audience and telling the story of the song. All exercises offered are meant to support the pedagogues. This does not mean the singers cannot perform them alone and thus develop their skills. It is important, however, to have an assessment by another person, so that the work done can be evaluated. This is the role of the pedagogue or a colleague who will watch you.

Auxiliary Exercises

The auxiliary exercises have nothing to do with the creative work of the singer and artist. They are not connected to the training material. These exercises are performed at the beginning and at the end of the lesson and aim at warming up (at the beginning) and relaxing (at the end). Exercise sets may be found in different works—on sports, pedagogy, theatre, health matters, etc. I will not discuss all types. I offer a set based on the following understanding: the major task of the auxiliary exercises is to warm up the body of the singer and actor uniformly and prepare it for the training process.

Please note: All exercises are performed without too much effort. Let us not forget that the goal is not a sports achievement. It is the preparation of the body for work without intense physical activity.

To begin with, we warm up the wrists, we make light, circle-like movements in both directions, 10 times in each. We continue with catch-like movements. Once again we make ten movements in each direction. The elbows come next. We perform circles to the left and right—10 times in each direction. The palms are clenched in fists. The same movements will follow, performed by the shoulders. Further, we continue warming up the shoulders with movements in front of the chest, with elbows closed while the palms are open like a knife. We open the hands in this position twice, then we open the hands again with the elbows open. This is one of the most popular exercises to warm up the body.

The next exercise is with the two hands standing vertically—one up and one down. The left hand goes up, the right hand down. The movement is backwards. The palms may be open or clenched. The elbows are fully open.

These exercises are followed by the ones for the head and the neck. We bend the head to the left and to the right in the direction of the shoulders—10 times in each direction. Then we make 10 turns of the head clockwise and 10 counterclockwise. Further, we bend the head 10 times to the chest and to the back. To warm up the face, we use mimic movements—we smile widely first, then move the lips forward to a kiss. Having done this 10 times, we lightly massage the forehead, the cheek bones, the cheeks and the chin.

We return to the body—the waist repeats the exercises for the neck. The hands are put on the waist. The legs are open at shoulder length.

The legs warm up, starting from the ankles. One leg steps on its toes and we make circles to the left and to the right with the ankle—10 times in each direction. Then we change the leg.

The next exercise needs some coordination skills: we lift one leg and bend the knee, the thigh being horizontal to the ground. We make circles—10 to the left and 10 to the right. Hands are on the waist. The balance must be steady. We perform the same with the other leg.

At the end we make 10 movements with each leg in the following manner: one leg is forward with the knee bent, the other leg is back and is as straight as it can be. The front leg steps on the whole foot, the back leg steps on the toes. The movements are made in the direction of the ground. The legs change their positions after 10 repetitions.

The warm-up must not be longer than 5 or 6 minutes and it must be followed by relaxing the muscles. To achieve this, we jump lightly with our body relaxed. Some shaking movements, coupled with the jumps—this is what is needed before the actual lesson starts. The body is now "awake" and ready to participate in the lesson. The muscles have warmed up and will be able to respond to the signals of the brain without hindrances or compensations.

Exercises Supporting the Stage Performance Study Process

The training in stage performance should be a creative process dependent on the pedagogue and the student. The same subject can never be taught the same way. This is why the exercises which I will suggest for the training process represent only the basis from which the pedagogue and the performer can start identifying the exercises and look for variants in each individual case. I split the exercises in two groups. The first is the group of studies which are short creative exercises and the second constitutes exercises which support the work on particular songs, the approach to specific training problems, etc.

Studies (Sketches)

These exercises include all those short acting assignments which educate and train the students to look for solutions of their own. In the initial stages of the training studies do not need to be long or contain dramaturgical elements.

Examples

1. Depict only with your body and face an object, an animal, a state. Use no words. The task may be developed further—use only your face, use only your body, do it with one hand only, etc.

The goal of the student in a similar sketch will be to develop how to react quickly in search of what will be most characteristic and will make everybody guess correctly the object described.

2. In the second case expressing an attitude will be added to the assignment of the first: show a candle which is burning and *happily* melting down.

   This is a creative task which aims at bringing forth emotions. That is, motion and attitude will mix together. The performer will again look for what is most characteristic in order to depict the burning and the melting of the candle, but will also convey emotions to us. An emotion we cannot see in an object which is slowly but surely ending its existence.

3. A "*Guess the Film*" game. This is a key exercise for group training. A trainee will explain only with gestures the title of a film. The rest will have to guess by asking questions which are answered by gestures alone by the trainee. This study may be performed by two persons or two groups. It may also be conducted as a competition. This exercise takes more time, but it is useful as there are more objects to be described and the person giving the explanations is pressed for time. The competitive aspect adds tension and trains the student's mind on his attempts to walk on stage in front of people and do things which he will not normally do when not on the stage. One of the most important features of this exercise is challenging the trainee not to make imprecise, parasitic movements.

4. One more exercise for advanced students: sing a song in different ways. That is, play the song, present it, change the position with which the singer-artist walks on the stage and "tells" the story. For example:

   - perform a modern dance song as an old lady would sing it. Probably, the manner of singing will change as the body may assume positions which are not convenient for singing;
   - do the same but as performed by an animal, by a man of a certain profession, etc.

Many more exercises and studies may be suggested for the development of the artistic capacities of singers. Several specialists have written on the subject. It is a matter of personal choice for the pedagogue and the singer to choose their way. It must be coordinated with the specific case and specific capacities. Also, it must be coordinated with the goals and tasks set for the team of pedagogues and students.

Auxiliary Effect Exercises

Quite often in practice the student faces a "block." He is unable to find a solution to a situation no matter how many times the pedagogue may have explained what needs to be done and how. Every trainer and trainee has been in a similar situation. Based on his experience, the pedagogue must find a way to stimulate the creative search, behavior and attitude of the student. He is the one who knows the "whats and hows." He is the leader. The student must follow in order to reach the goal. I offer several exercises for critical moments which may help both student and teacher.

Please note: this part of the exercise must be done with the assistance of a pedagogue. It is he who will judge what is to be done and how, when we are successful and when we are not. This is why I am talking about exercises in the process of training and not in the process of *self*-training.

What is the problem with the phrase "I am doing it! What more do I need to do?" This response is due to the lack of feedback. The student does not see what he is doing, but believes he does so exactly as he should. If the trainee has been instructed multiple times and no change follows, the pedagogue must be there to suggest an alternative method or way to solve the issue of the feedback and of the meaning of his specific requirements. The best way to do this is to use a mirror. Practice has proven that singing in front of a mirror can be as useful as it is dangerous. We are talking about a big mirror in which the student can see himself at full height or at least three fourths. The small mirror which is used at the initial stages of singing studies is not discussed here. Its purpose is to improve the training of the voice.

The use of the big mirror must be done at certain intervals. They depend on how often the student needs to see himself to understand that he is not doing things the way the trainer wants him to. The danger of singing in front of the mirror comes from the students forgetting that the mirror reflects them and they start expecting "something to happen in the mirror." Staring at the mirrored image leads to forgetting the main tasks and to distraction. A video recording is the alternative to the use of a mirror. In these times of high technology everyone has a cellphone with a camera. It is, however, necessary that the quality of the video recording be good enough to show clearly who does what. For this purpose we need to use a camera which is a camera ONLY and is on a stand. In this way neither the student nor the pedagogue would be distracted by taking care of the technical aspects. The stand offers one more advantage: there is nothing else that can distract tutor and pupil as the student is free to do what he likes and concentrate on honing his skills. He can surmount whatever obstacles he may have along the road to learning and developing his stage performance skills. We need to note that often there will be no audience in the course of the rehearsal process. This makes the assignment more complicated as the singer cannot get a feedback on the spot, he cannot see how he is doing. The feedback comes later on in three ways—by the video recording, by the opinion of the pedagogue or by the two combined.

I call the next exercise "Tell the story only with your face." The student and the pedagogue, or two students, the student and a friend sit against each other on chairs or stools, at both sides of the table or desk, or on a sofa, the steps of the proscenium or the podium—it does not matter where. You may perform the exercise standing too, but sitting is preferable. What is important is that the body will be at rest, the hands—relaxed, doing nothing. Just the way you sit at a bar or have coffee. The hands are busy with the cups or something else, but do not move or take part in the conversation.

The singer starts to sing. It is better if at the beginning it is a cappella. The singer tells the story to one single person—his interlocutor. The exercise is repeated by singing again the first couplet—as many times as necessary for the student to understand the task and to manifest results. The task is to move the face muscles so that the mimic muscles will start working and participate in the creation of the character. The eyes, the movements of the neck, the eyebrows, the smile—they must all be very actively part of the presentation of the song.

At the second stage the student stands up, having understood the assignment and using actively the mimic muscles depending on the song context. In this way he guides the body into participation and the work of the face and the head follows. This exercise is useful for the mimic muscles in the case of performers with no active facial expressions. It can be also used for shy people. The result can be quite rewarding, but you should not expect it to turn into a panacea for all problems. Shyness will not go away, for example.

In another exercise the student sings his song and simultaneously does things which have nothing to do with it: juggling, balancing a stick, arranging objects, throwing and catching a ball, etc. The purpose is to eliminate any traces of selfconciousness so that he will start performing the song without thinking about singing and behavior.

The following exercise is similar in content and different in physical activity. We can say it is a mixture of the previous two. The student starts singing a song and walks around the hall with the pedagogue or with another person. They imitate walking in the park. The student tells the story to his partner and controls the pace, the moments of stopping, starting again, etc. The purpose is for the student to feel he is in familiar circumstances, so that he is not distracted by thinking what to do with his hands. The two being close to each other allows the student to find the balance—how many times and how often to look the other in the eye, as well as how long the look should be. The veracity of what is happening depends on that—whether they really are in the park and are walking. Besides setting free the hands and the body, the exercise does one more thing: it shows to the student that if his movements are natural in the specific circumstances, he will not worry and will do everything the right way. It is good if the pedagogue reacts with his face and hands to the words and movements of the student in the course of the exercise. This will be a dialogue. The pedagogue should also follow the student's non-verbal directions on the place to stop, the duration of the stop, the speed of walking and other natural events which may occur in the course of a walk in the park.

Here is the last exercise which is probably the most difficult: sing a sad song in a way to make it a comic one without changing the manner of singing and the meaning of the lyrics. So far we have already offered a very clear hint—the lyrics must not be changed *verbally*. What the author created will be preserved as it is! The meaning will be changed by non-verbal means. For example, a city transport bus driver who drives the vehicle and sells tickets will be the singer. A flat tyre or a road accident may occur. The dramaturgy of the lyrics and the dramaturgy of what is happening need to correlate in a way so that the important moments, the moments of accent in the song will coincide with the accents of the acting assignment. If a pedestrian crosses the street at a red traffic light and the driver jerks the bus, this moment in the song must coincide with a declaration of love, an acceptance of a marriage proposal—it may be anything. If we add to that a gesture characteristic of the driver's world, it would be funny.

To sum up: once again I would like to stress that the above exercises are basic. You should use them as examples and invent your own, matching your needs as a trainer or trainee. I need to add: you should not count on exercises solving all issues of stage performance training. The life experience of the pedagogue-and-student team, their personal qualities and erudition, their education, other interests, free creative thinking and many more factors will count as they all play a role in the development of the student. Last but not least will come the talent, perseverance and efficiency of both participants in the process which we call training. Both must reach a level of artistry which for an onlooker will seem as easy as a child's play. Behind that will be years of hard work. There is no easy solution on how to attain the high goals set.

Relaxation Exercises and Closing the Lesson

For this part of the lesson yoga or sports exercises may be used. You may also just sit down after the analysis of the lesson and stay quiet for a while. Let the tension ebb away! Let the trainee and the trainer tune up to a final or next lesson or any other job. They must not part ways abruptly. They must leave the character and the learning process and the burden of the new material should stay in the hall.

The exercises are varied, starting with breathing ones—circular movements of the hands up to meditative ones—standing still. The body may simply relax and by small jumps "shake off" the tension. The basic purpose, I repeat, is to unload the tension accumulated during the lesson. Whether it had been positive or negative, the tension has its positive and negative aspects.

One last piece of advice: before starting the relaxation exercises it is good to close the lesson by something easy and already learnt by the student. The goal is for the lesson to leave a good feeling. Something well done and successful will be well remembered. If that is done, the relaxation exercises and the follow-up actions of both the student and the pedagogue will carry forward the positive emotions of the last task and its good performance. When the lesson has been successful and I am satisfied with the work done, I take the hands of the student in mine to form a cross. In the case of a group—we form a circle together. I thank all for the lesson well done and then we separate.

Some Advice

I will share some thoughts as advice. These have come from practice and have arisen as a result of issues which had to be solved quickly or immediately. They may also be simple things we do not think about often and omit in practical activities. The advice part is quite short and it aims at making you think and discover some solutions on your own.

If you do not have a mirror in the rehearsal hall, record a video and analyze it! Analyze mercilessly every second, every movement recorded! Listen to the real masters of artistry in the voice, listen to Lara Fabian, Elvis Presley (his late ballads), Freddie Mercury, Michael Jackson, Robbie Williams and others.

Enter the studio well prepared with the music and the lyrics. Quite often you forget your materials for no apparent reason. It is fine to have a sheet of paper in front of you, to look at it, write down something, or just keep it in order to stay calm.

An exercise to avoid being startled by technical issues? There is no such exercise, but there is experience instead. There are habits. Create your own habits and when you are stressed, resort to them. Rehearse with both your hands free and when you have the mike, one hand will simply hold it, the other will gesticulate! This will happen naturally. You may not believe it, but that's how it is.

Work on good articulation in the official literary language! Read aloud and as written in the books. Do not let yourself be misled by the widely-accepted practice to think that you can do anything and talk in any way: using dialect forms, soft or hard pronunciations, behave impolitely or disrespectfully to the audience.

Do your homework in front of the mirror—do that every 4 or 5 rehearsals, so that you do not become inured to your own reflection. To reiterate the point, you need to practice in front of the mirror so you can watch and analyze your performance. But the habit of looking at the left and right part of the audience may be lost. *Be careful with the mirror*!

Your stage fever needs to subside before you step on the stage. The techniques are individual, but if needed, ask for a place where you can be alone for a while, ask for some water or fruits to be brought to you, make yourself comfortable and cozy. You are the star! You can also do some breathing exercises. Go through the "risky" moments of your program.

What if the audience does not react the way you wish them to? You can stop and do something to catch their attention. Start a game or make them clap rhythmically. Doing that needs experience and courage! Do it carefully!

Gestures may not mean the same thing in different cultural circumstances and thus may be understood differently. If you have to participate in a concert or be part of a competition, get some information about local traditions and specific gestures. Quite often you may go to a neighboring country and fall into a funny or embarrassing situation if you are not aware that some gestures may be considered offensive there. Some professional or social groups may have their own specific gestures, used for communication inside the group. Divers, for instance, would be a typical example. We need to know some basic gestures if we want to impress the audience during a concert tour. In this way we will not discredit ourselves!

If you do not know what to do with your hands—do nothing! Yes, let them hang free at the sides and do not put them in your pockets or hold the mike with both hands!

When working with the camera, think of the camera as an interlocutor. Do not be afraid of it!

Conclusion

This work is based on some theoretical search in the field of stage art, body language, communication, training, sound technique, as well as on practice in the training of singers and actors in private education and in the state educational system, not to forget the personal experience of the author. The selection of the subject was arrived at after years of observance and participation in contemporary show business at home and abroad. While observing and analyzing the behavior and communication skills of the actors and singers, both amateur and professional, it was only natural to come to the question: "Why can some of them communicate with the audience and manage it while others cannot?"

Several basic points can be formulated when studying this book in detail. In the first place, the course can be used as the basis for training in verbal and non-verbal communication. It is the first of its kind, being organized in setting short and long term goals and tasks, exercises, studies, advice. Experts in the field are rare. Hence there is only a small amount of literature on the subject. The absence of similar works in educational literature at the national and international level is definitely a loss for both future singers and actors as well for their pedagogues.

Thus, without claiming to be comprehensive, this book is a pioneering one and sets the reference points for other researchers to follow. It lays the foundation and turns the complex synthesis of varied knowledge and skills into a system, formulates clear directions and approaches how to work with all the elements of the art of singing as far as stage performance and the verbal and non-verbal communication with the audience go.

I need to note that because of the lack of specialized works in the field this book can serve as a guide or a kind of easily accessible literature to assist the efforts of pedagogues in the field. By providing clear and specific information on a number of issues this reference book can assist both professionals in stage performance and audience communication as well as vocal pedagogues, who probably cannot contact other experts. A number of new concepts have been introduced: the singing body, the phrase in the gesture, the phrase in the look, etc.

Every singer and artist, pedagogue or amateur singer may add their knowledge and elaborate on what has been written. They may disagree; they may suggest an alternative solution to a pedagogical problem. By the fact of its existence this book may undoubtedly raise questions, provoke different opinions and perhaps disputes. This will be proof that its role is to be out there and stimulate the desire in pedagogues and students either to train or to exercise in verbal and non-verbal communication, to use it in a controlled manner and manage the audience through it. Further, they will understand the audience messages sent in response to their performance, will be able to "break" and change the negative attitude vis-a-vis themselves, and create a new and better quality level of their reputation. To become actors who are perfectly aware of what they do on stage, actors who fully understand their message and how to share it with the audience.

The purpose of this work is by means of the pedagogue to wake up the body of the singer and artist and turn it into a "singing body." This is the body which will tell stories together with the voice. The body which is a full participant in the process of the stage presentation of the work of pedagogues and students of vocal art in all genres and styles.

This is a new piece of work which steps on other scientific, pedagogical and creative practices and processes. It opens a new niche by not simply pointing out to it, but also by providing guidelines on how and in what directions this avenue should be developed by future pedagogues so that they occupy their own place in the verbal and non-verbal communication of the singer and artist with the audience.

Bibliography

1. Pease, B., Pease, A. *The Definitive Book of Body Language: The Hidden Meaning Behind People's Gestures and Expressions*. Random House, 2008.
2. Pease, A., Garner, A. *Talk Language: How to Use Conversation for Profit and Pleasure*. Orion Publishing, 2002.
3. Morris, D. *Bodytalk: The Meaning of Human Gestures*. Crown Publishing, 1995.
4. Morris, D. *Manwatching: A Field Guide to Human Behavior*. Harry N. Abrams, 1979.
5. Navarro, J., Karlins, M. *What Every BODY is Saying: An Ex-FBI Agent's Guide to Speed-Reading People*. HarperCollins, 2009.
6. Argyle, M. *Bodily Communication*, L, 1978.
7. Carlson. R. *What Do I Do With My Hands?: A Guide to Acting for the Singers*. Personal Dynamics Publishing, 2013.
8. Duncan, S. Nonverbal communication. *Psychological Bulletin*, 1969, 72(2), 118–137.
9. Nicholson, S. *Ella Fitzgerald: A Biography of the First Lady of Jazz*. Indigo, London, 1996.
10. Scheflen, A. *Human Territories: How We Behave in Space-time*. Prentice Hall, New Jersey, 1976.
11. Schuller, G. *Early Jazz: It's Roots and Musical Development*. Oxford University Press, New York, 1968.
12. Ward, G. *Jazz: A History of America's Music*. Knopf, New York, 2000.
13. "Работа актера над ролью" К.С. Станиславский.
14. "Алгоритъм на звучащото слово," Любомир Гърбев.
15. Гърбев, Л. Образи зад думите, София: НБУ, 1999.
16. Дафов, Ан. Народнопесенният изпълнителски стил и неговите вокално-педагогически проблеми. Музика, С, 1978.
17. Дмитриев, Л. Голосовой аппарат певца. Музыка, М, 1964.
18. Жекова, К. Практическа вокална методика. МАФК, Пловдив (второ издание).

19. Заседателев, Ф. Научньй основьй постановки голоса. Музгиз, М, 1937.
20. Иванов, Ал.П. Об исскустве пения. Музгиз, М, 1993.
21. Йосифов, И. Трудният път към голямото певческо изкуство. Музика, С, 1992.
22. Рупчев, Й./Хофман, Х. АБВ на поп музиката. Музика, С, 1987.
23. Карагьозов, Хр. "Микрофони—видове и спецификация": Лекция на д.т.н. Хр. Карагьозов пред студентите в СУ, 05.11.2014.
24. Каринч, М и Хартли Гр. Езикът на жестовете. Издателство "Кръгозор" 2009.
25. Квинтилиан, М. Ф. Обучението на оратора. С, 1999.
26. Киселова, Е. За вокалната педагогика. Наука и изкуство, С, 1963.
27. Константинов, В. Театърът през погледа на Бертолт Брехт. Електронно издателство "LitertNet," 2005.
28. Кушлева, А. Звукоизвличане и орнаментика при народното пеене. Методи за тяхното овладяване. Университетско издание, Пловдив, 1996.
29. Лабунская,В.Невербальноеповедение(Социально-перцептивный подход), Ростов на Дону, 1986.
30. Ламперти, Фр. Исскуство пения. Музсектор, М, 1923.
31. Луканин, В. Обучение и воспитание молодого певца. Музгиз, М, 1977.
32. Люки, Р. Коучинг и менторство. Издателство "Класика и Стил," 2008.
33. Михалева, Ср. Вокална техника. Университетско издателство "Св. Св.Кирил и Методий," В. Търново, 2006.
34. Морис, Д. Жестове и поведение. Издателство "Сиела," 2007.
35. Наваро, Дж. и Карлис М. Какво казва тялото. Издателство "Изток—Запад," 2011.
36. Назаренко, И. Изкуството на пеенето. Наука и изкуство, С, 1975.
37. Органов, П. Гласът на певеца и методика на неговата постановка. Наука иизкуство, С, 1955.
38. Орукин, Е. От нешколувания тон до високото певческо майсторство. Наука и изкуство, С, 1963.
39. Пенчева, Ел. Невербални техники за повишаване на комуникативните умения. В сб. Методи за работа в малка група, С, 1995.

40. Петрова, Н.И. Индивидиальный стиль деятельности учителя, Казан, 1982.
41. Пийз, Алън, Алън Гарнър. Езикът на тялото. Скритият смисъл на думите. С, 2000.
42. Работнов, Л. Голос и речь. Статьи в БСЕ и БМЕ, М, 1929.
43. Райнов, В. Символното поведение на човека, С, 1993.
44. Регуш, Л., Иванов, Ст., Иванов, М. Наблюдателността във всекидневното общуване, С, 1994.
45. Руменчев, В. Невербалната комуникация в ораторското изкуство, С, 1988.
46. Руменчев, В. Несловесното общуване в ораторското изкуство, С, 1985.
47. Руменчев, В. Съдебна реторика, С, 1997.
48. Станиславски, К.С. Работата на актьора върху ролята. Издателство "Наука и Изкуство," 1977.
49. Стателова, Р./Чендов, Ч. Поп музиката. Музика, С, 1983.
50. Синтова, А. Вокална постановка.
51. Стоицова, Т. Живеем с другите, С, 1998.
52. Стоицова, Т. И усмивката може да бъде заповед, С, 1992.
53. Стойков, Л. Фирмена култура и комуникация, С, 1995, стр. 145–155.
54. Тоцева, Я. Етнокултурни особености на някои елементи на невербалното поведение. В сб. Интеркултурни взаимодействия. Съставител: Ив. Иванов, Шумен, 1997.
55. Тоцева, Я. Особености на жестикулацията при основните етноси. В сб. Етнокултурен диалог на Балканите, София, 2001, стр. 437–447.
56. Фаст, Дж. Езикът на тялото, С, 1993.
57. Чехов, М. Тайны актерского мастерства. ООО "Издательство АСТ," Москва, Россия, 2010.
58. Чешко, О. Певческий голос и его свойства, 1999.
59. Юсон, Р. Певческий голос, 1974.
60. Адамс, С. За джаза накратко. Рива, С, 2010.
61. Андреева, Л. Социално познание и междуличностно взаимодействие. С, 1999.
62. Апресян, Г. З. Ораторското изкуство. С, 1970, стр. 122–126.

63. Аргайл, М., М. Хендерсън. Анатомия на човешките отношения, С, 1989.
64. Аспелунд, Д. Развитие певца и его голоса. Музгиз, М, 1952.
65. Боварян, А. Вокално-постановъчна работа в жанровата музика. Аскони, С, 2007.
66. Бошева, Майя К. Сценично поведение на студентите—бъдещи поп певци.
67. Брехт, Б. Малък органон за театъра, 1948–1954, Електронно издателство "LitertNet," 2006.
68. Брехт, Б. Диалектиката в театъра, 1951–1955, Електронно издателство "LitertNet," 2009.
69. Брехт, Б. Избрани творби в четири тома. Том 4. Размисли върху театъра и литературата. "Народна култура," 1983.
70. Вискът, Д. Езикът на чувствата. С, 1993.
71. Георгиев, Л. Евъргрийни на всички времена. С, 1993.
72. Глас, Л. Знам какво си мислиш. С, 2003.
73. Грозева, В. Срещи с имена на джаза. Музика, С, 1982.

Index

For Product Safety Concerns and Information please contact our EU representative GPSR@taylorandfrancis.com
Taylor & Francis Verlag GmbH, Kaufingerstraße 24, 80331 München, Germany

www.ingramcontent.com/pod-product-compliance
Lightning Source LLC
LaVergne TN
LVHW020635100826
845148LV00012B/2193

* 9 7 8 9 8 1 4 8 0 0 2 0 4 *